Ask, Don't Tell

Six Easy Steps to Improving Communication, Self-Control and Interpersonal Relationships

By Dr. Dianne Olvera

ISBN 0-7414-4195-0

Published by:

INFI∞ITY
PUBLISHING.COM

1094 New DeHaven Street, Suite 100
West Conshohocken, PA 19428-2713
Info@buybooksontheweb.com
www.buybooksontheweb.com
Toll-free (877) BUY BOOK
Local Phone (610) 941-9999
Fax (610) 941-9959

Printed in the United States of America

Printed on Recycled Paper

Published September 2007

Foreword

This book was written at the request of many of my clients because they used the information contained in this book to help them attain a new way of conversing. All noted that it helped improve their interpersonal relationships. They wanted to know more and more about how to use each step. Hence, the idea for this material grew from both my personal as well as my private practice experiences. Names and situations have been changed to protect the confidential information of my clients.

Since I started developing this technique many years ago, it has been nice to see how many clients have changed their lives for the better. These same people are now using the information provided in this book to help their own friends, colleagues and family members take control of their lives and become more positive people. Parents noted that they started using InterActive speech with their very young children and have reduced power struggles and temper tantrums. They continue using this technique with all their children, no matter the age because it permitted their children to make their own choices, resulting in less conflict with them. Doing so places responsibility on the child rather than the parent. Parents of teenagers are finding that they have less power struggles because they are now able to talk "with" their children rather than "to" them. This interchange of ideas helps the parents to understand their teenage children's wants and needs so that they can facilitate communication with young people in the various stages of transition from childhood to adulthood.

These successful family interactions carried over to the workplace and into adult relationships resulting in improved business ventures as well as social-emotional opportunities. Overall, success using InterActive speech has been had by all who work through the various steps to achieve successful communication. I urge anyone with a sincere desire to stop arguing to read this book. One can finally achieve peace of mind knowing that the words we used are actually heard and acted on. May you finally achieve the peace, kindness and confidence you have always longed for through the ideas found in my book.

I'd like to thank my husband, our community book club, especially Janet, Laura and friends for their help and support throughout this interesting journey.

Sincerely yours,

Dianne L. Olvera, Ph.D., BCET
Educational Therapist and Professor

Contents

How InterActive Speech Was Derived

As I collected information on different types of verbal exchanges, I found myself reflecting back on my childhood to find out why my parents always fought. Even as a child I couldn't understand why one family got along so well while another family's dynamics were so volatile. These interactions always intrigued me and I often looked for answers in the typical places such as family background, aggressive personalities, and interpersonal differences as reasons why relationships fell apart. I never stopped to realize that it was really the way they used their words that resulted in a calm and loving interaction or a spontaneous cat fight that ended with angry and sometimes emotional and physical repercussions.

My curiosity spanned many areas of the world as I moved from the United Stated in 1971 and lived in Buenos Aires, Argentina for 10 years. While living in Argentina, I worked as a teacher and married my American husband who was a diplomat with the United States Embassy. While there, we interacted with people from all over Latin America and who came from diverse age and social economic brackets. Our next assignment was in Mexico City to represent the United States Air Force at social engagements and gather information on topics and people from around the world. Our mode of gathering that information was through verbal interactions. I noticed that, no matter what language the people spoke, words or the lack of them were the basis of comfortable or difficult social and personal interactions. Most common were the words that people did **not** use that often resulted in situations that got them into trouble because the intention the speaker had in mind when the words were spoken did not always match the interpretation the listener got when those words were heard.

Finally it came to me. I needed to stop looking at the source of each person's interpersonal strengths or weaknesses and focus on just what came out of each person's mouth. I also focused on how they used their eyes and how they expressed themselves through body language. From an untrained eye, I thought these forms of observational research had no theory or formal foundation. However, when we returned to the United States, I entered my Master's program in bilingual special education to learn more about this subject. Learning the theories of language acquisition and the cultural nuances behind interpersonal communication was fascinating. These courses were so fascinating that I went on to complete all the prerequisites for my doctorate in the programs for bilingual special education and administration. However, when I got ready to work on my dissertation in bilingual special education, I decided I needed a new perspective to help me complete all facets of language interaction and communication. Therefore, I entered a second doctorial program.

This time my focus was on Language, Reading, and Culture. This was a relatively new program at the University of Arizona and was taught by experts from a variety of academic domains. Although my studies encompassed many authors and theories, one person and his theories stood out above the rest, Lev S. Vygotsky (1896-1934). He was best described by Stephen Toulmin (1990) as a man who was:

> Freed from the constraints which the combination of pragmatism and behaviorism have tended to place on experimental psychology, Vygotsky was able to start from the study of Shakespeare and move easily across most of cognitive and developmental psychology to the brink of neuropsychology. In doing so, he explored the whole area between literary theory, neurology and psycholinguistics with extraordinary freedom. Only in the last thirty years have the subtlety and fruitfulness of his work begun to be appreciated fully by people in the West. (Stephen Toulmin, Avalon Professor of Humanities, Northwestern University reflects

on Alex Kozulin's book *Vygotsky's psychology: A biography of ideas).*

Given the multidimensional perspectives discussed in the classes related to Vygotsky's, as well as through private discussions with Dr. Luis Moll, one of my dissertation advisors who was an expert on Vygotsky's work, opened my eyes not only to the universality of how we use our language, but also to the impact it has on our individual development.

My next step was to go out into the community and put some of these theories to work and use that information to determine how change can take place through appropriate use of interpersonal language. Since educational change within the classroom was an area of need in my community, I chose to work with a group of teachers in a school where some international students were housed. Common to the work I proposed for these teachers (who ranged in age and experience from novice to pre-retirement), was research that grew out of the Kamehameha Elementary Education Program (KEEP) in Hawaii. This research was headed by Roland G. Tharp and Ronald Gallimore from the University of California. Their work, called Instructional Conversation consisted of ten elements. Five of these elements were devoted to helping teachers organize their teaching in an interactive way so that students would have more input in the teaching/learning process. The next five elements were devoted to helping teachers use their words to help students move from a teacher-directed mode to a student-centered mode. Using this form of classroom discourse helped students assimilate more information and attain a deeper level of understanding of the course content. The basic format encouraged teachers to stop "telling" students what to do and start engaging in real communication through questions and discussions.

My initial observations in the research teachers' classrooms afforded me the opportunity to view traditional instructional methods where the teacher was the source of information and the students were the receivers of their commands.

Conversations between teacher and student were limited to instruction on course material and directions on how their seatwork was to be completed. No attention was paid to how the student felt or reacted to the lesson. Task completion was the sole purpose and any discussion related to the instructional topic was considered a waste of time in an already overloaded instructional day. But I kept wondering if learning actually took place.

When I asked the teachers to move beyond the traditional instructional format and involve the students in discussions, my goals were quickly dismissed. Lack of time was the common rationale for not conversing, but as I worked with these teachers I began to realize that it was even harder to get the teachers to express their own feelings about this new research and why they felt they could not implement it in their instruction. I noticed that they all felt uncomfortable with the "act" of discussion. Most noted that they had difficulty expressing their personal thoughts, let alone attend to the comments of students. They mostly feared they would not have a response to their student's questions or comments and would therefore lose control of the behavior in the classroom.

Obviously, convincing teachers to do something that they have never had in their own educational experiences was a difficult task. Added to this difficulty was the lack of personal verbiage to express themselves as individuals and as a group. Together, both pieces seemed like a paramount impediment to overcome.

Therefore, I began to use the interpersonal perspectives I urged the teachers to use with their students as a means of being a role-model to the teachers in my research. At first, they were taken back at my questions and my desire to hear them talk rather than just stand in the front of the room and pose ideas and expect them to be completed in the classroom. Fostering communication was a very difficult task because the old habits of "telling" kids what to do was strongly ingrained in each teacher's methodology. Hence, there was much intimidation and fear of losing that ever-so-precious classroom control that needed to be overcome before we could make any headway with the instructional change posed for this research.

At times, some of the teachers wanted to go back to their comfort zones of traditional teaching. However, the saving grace came when their students started to take a personal interest in their own learning. Surprisingly, even the least interested and unmotivated students started to become active learners! When the sparks started to fly and students questioned rather than passively accepted the curricular content, the teachers knew they would never return to their previous style of teaching. Follow-up communication with the teachers showed that all continued using this instructional format.

The success of this research spurred me to continue my work with a large school district where I oversaw a legal issue involving a dispute between the rich and poor areas of the polarized school district. Even within the district office, many departments would not interact with each other. The Native Americans felt they were not understood; the Black Studies group felt that they were the minority voices; and the Bilingual group felt that they were not appreciated. Rather than express their differences openly during inter-group discussions, each group resided in their distinct posts and came together only when necessary. Often issues of common concern were stalemated by the group's failure to agree on agendas because each person had a different perspective on how their cultural group should be addressed.

These interpersonal cultural rifts went on for years and were never openly addressed, and being the new person on staff, I was not privy to the historical backgrounds of each group. Therefore, I innocently entered the scene with all the enthusiasm of a new graduate student. That enthusiasm soon burst during a cultural group discussion where I observed all the idiosyncrasies that existed within and between departments. When I asked how their problems could be remedied, all answered that it was an impossible task because the precedence had been set and no one could change many years of interdepartmental rift.

At meetings where all departments were together, I would observe how people talked to each other. I also took note of how both cultural and social nuances either helped or hindered interpersonal relationships. I studied which people were open and which ones held their feelings closed up inside them. Over time, I started to delve into the thinking process of each person by just asking simple, open-ended questions. I would often listen to what someone would say at a meeting and, when we were in a subsequent private meeting, I would ask something like, "Why did you feel that the discussion leader was prejudiced against your group?" "What words did that person use that made you and your group feel uncomfortable?" Then, I did something that few remember to do – I waited and listened to what that person had to say. After carefully listening, I would take the last thing they said and use that as my next opening question or reply, Here is an example of one conversation.

Department Head: The discussion leader told us that our teachers were out of line when they permitted the students to talk and dance during their class time; however, that is a cultural difference and they won't accept *our* way of presenting curriculum."

My response: "If you felt that the cultural differences between your group and that of the discussion leader were not understood, why not present that information in a way that will help the leader learn more about your culture's preferred form of instruction and define how that format could enhance student learning?"

This simple question led that group to put on a presentation about cultural nuances at our next meeting. The presentation emphasized the role culture plays in the learning process and all invited came away from that meeting with a greater understanding of the impact culture played in learning as well as how different behaviors could be interpreted by someone outside of that particular culture.

This step opened the door for further inter-cultural explorations and, more importantly, helped open the door for dialogue to take place through acceptance of each other's cultural differences. Over time, differences were minimized which afforded greater assistance to the diverse youth in the whole district. Also, a more cohesive working relationship prevailed within and between departments at the district office.

The aforementioned scenario shows how such a slight change in the way we express ourselves can make a huge impact on our working environment as well as on our interpersonal lives.

After a few years in this position, my husband was transferred to Florida and I took part-time teaching positions at a few universities in Boca Raton, Florida. I also opened a private practice with a psychiatrist and worked with many families who had diverse learning and behavior problems. I often attended to children diagnosed as having a nonverbal learning disability commonly known as NLD. These children have autistic-like behaviors where they do not see social nuances and experience difficulty working with abstract information. My interests led me to approach the Complex Systems and Brain Sciences group on campus to see if they would accept my students for MRI and fMRI studies. My goal was to determine if verbal mediation also called self-talk, had any effect on the way we process information. Therefore, we took a small group of my students and some of my parents and studied the effect touching fingers in a certain pattern had on brain processing. The NLD students had activity in many areas of the brain when they first tried the finger-tap procedure. However, once we gave each finger a number and asked them to redo the patterns using the spoken pattern we found little difference in brain processing when compared with the norm group. (*The Influence of Instruction Modality on Brain Activation in Teenagers with Nonverbal Learning Disabilities: Two Case Histories* 2007: Journal of Learning Disabilities)

This research study helped me understand that brain activity was changed when verbal mediation was used. Therefore, I continued to perfect a methodology that was logical and easy to use. I taught the children and their parents to learn about their own wiring so that they were able to then define their specific wants and needs. It worked both in and out of school and families were able to enjoy their children again!

The final piece of this personal history came when we moved to California and my university students and clients kept asking for a book to read with directions on how to use the process I prescribed in my office. Hence, this book was born.

InterActive Speech Defined

As an educational therapist and university professor, I have had the opportunity to watch the impact words have on people. I have also noted how we use our words to empower or rob other people of their power.

While working with families in my private practice, I kept reminding parents to stop taking the words away from their children each time they talked. One day, a parent asked why the words she spoke played such an important role in interpersonal relationships. That's when I realized that I was trying to get the parents to observe the reaction their words had on their children. As I pondered the process longer, I came to the conclusion that conversations are really "inter" (within and between people) and – in order for both parties to be equal participants they both needed to take an "active" role in the conversation. Therefore, the term "Inter-Active" speech was born!

Simplistically defined, Inter-Active speech involves determining the end result you are expecting from that conversation before you engage in it. For example, I want my husband to take more responsibility helping out around the house. Then, working backward, you can attain this goal by asking questions and listening to the reply given by my husband. As I "Actively" listen to what my husband says, I can determine how I want to use one, two, or more of the steps outlined in this book to attain my desired goal without fighting or animosity. The most used step "Ask, Don't Tell" became the title of this book because it is the underlying premise of most conversational interactions. If we spend more time asking questions in order to define what we heard as well as clarify comments that were implied or not clear, we will be able to carry on conversations that have substance and meaning while encountering fewer fights and frustrations.

People have asked me how our society got to this place of language discord. I tell them that internal speech (or talking to oneself) actually starts shortly after birth. Crib talk is an example of how children learn to self-mediate (tell yourself what to do or what not to do). Self-talk is also a means of using your own words to help soothe your emotions and calm yourself when you are feeling frustrated or scared. We live in a fast-paced society and our days are jam-packed movement from the time we get up until the time we fall into bed at night. Therefore, we have gotten into the habit of condensing our words to directives rather than conversations. Even as we are relaxing, we are multi-tasking, and with the onset of the computer and instant messaging, our language has diminished even more. So, to answer the question of how we got to this place, we can all answer – we are just not taking the time to stop, talk and more importantly listen! Asking, rather than just commanding and telling others will help our society regain the sense of community because we are actually using our words to attain clarity of thought. Clarity of thought results in clarity of mind. Clarity of mind results in being in control of our thoughts and the end result is control over our life.

The following story is an example of how our quick-paced lives usurp the quality in interpersonal communication.

Ever wonder how our rapid lifestyles effect our parenting and interpersonal techniques? Think about the reactions we have when a baby cries. The quickest remedy is to pick the baby up and calm him or her so that we can go on with our other tasks. After we have other children, we will have the older children attend to the younger ones so that we can live more comfortably in our already stressed-out world.

Research has shown that, if babies are picked up as soon as they feel uncomfortable, they will not have an opportunity to practice using their own problem solving strategies. These include hearing their voices when they need to self-soothe their emotions, or distracting themselves with their own babbling to make them happy. As babies get older and they start toddling around, young children will need to determine how to work through challenging situations such as getting the ball from under the couch. Children who are accustomed to figuring out their own problems will often be heard talking to themselves. The Toddler Story is a great example of this process.

The Toddler Stories

Toddler: "Oh, ball go."

Toddler: [bends over and sees the ball stuck under the couch] "Ball gone – oops!"

[Toddler gets down on his tummy and puts his hand under the couch until he touches the ball. Then he grabs it and pulls it out.] "Ha Ha! Ball!"

This short story shows how the toddler used his own words to define a problem, solve it and emotionally congratulate himself after he found his ball.

Now let's imagine the same situation with a child who is not comfortable figuring out his own problems:

Toddler: "Ball go!" Whaaaaaaaaaa!

Older brother: "Did you loose your ball? Here (brother hands the child the ball) – now stop crying."

The first scenario took place and no one in the family may have even known what transpired because the toddler figured out what to do and attended to his own problem without any assistance. His satisfied laugh when he found the ball shows how he gave himself positive feedback for his ability to overcome a challenge. This opportunity raised his self-esteem and helped him gain the confidence that he could overcome difficult situations.

The second situation, on the other hand, resulted in getting the job done. The toddler's cries for help were answered and someone else came to his aide by retrieving the ball for the baby. Although the older brother's gesture seemed innocent and simple, the lesson the baby learned was that other people will have to assist him because he is not capable of attending to his own needs unless he has help.

Although this is one small situation that can happen in any household, if the assistance continues over time, the assisted toddler can become dependent on others to help him succeed and to comfort him when he fails. Using others to provide assistance and comfort creates a learned helpless situation where the child believes that he can't succeed on his own.

Take this situation a step further and note how the young child who spends his early years around caring and over-attentive family members who talk him or her through each difficult situation at home or with family members. Then think about what will happen when the child is confronted with a situation on the playground or in the classroom and that older sibling or parent is not there to assist? Usually, this over-attended to child will not have the successful vocabulary and problem solving background to call on as examples to help him/her work through difficult situations. Over time, these people will often rely on others to interpret their needs and wants. When something does not result as intended, they may blame others rather than themselves for failure. For example, "I could not get to work on time because my dad forgot to set my alarm clock." Failure becomes the fault of others and not seen as the result of their own doing. The worker could have set his/her own alarm clock but, it never occurred to that person because he/she never had to do that in life. Therefore, it is obvious to the worker that the person at fault was the father because he did not arrange for him to get to work on time.

If we look at the aforementioned situation from both sides, we can see how the worker really feels that he/she is not to blame because the father has always taken control of that person's life, and with the control came the responsibility to take care of his/her own needs. From the father's perspective, his child has grown up to be a lazy, irresponsible person with no drive, motivation or self-worth.

All of these terms are true but, who helped these people get to where they are today?

Over my many years of practice, I have found that people who have difficulty expressing their own needs or calming their own feelings are often people who have been raised by parents and/or caregivers who provide a multitude of assistance. The over-doting parent or caregiver tends to rob the child of language and personal soothing because they pick up the baby as soon as she cries and soothes her with their own words when problems arise. The over-protective parent or guardian will also spend the formative years "telling" the child what to do and how to do it.

This type of person could have been raised by a busy parent who, for lack of time or patience, will do for the child and tell the child what to do in order to get life moving quickly throughout the day. By the time the child becomes a young adult, these parents will be worn down and frustrated because their children do not do anything on their own without being told or yelled at.

The bad news is that many of you can relate to these situations; however, the GOOD NEWS is that we can attain change at any age in our lives! In my own life, I have used the six steps with all age groups in many different environments with successful change. Gone are the days of beating myself up over being the slave to my friends, family, students and co-workers.

If you don't relate to the aforementioned situations, you might want to think about, how often have you felt powerless when someone interrupts your thoughts and conversation to take over your words? Do you feel as though that person has just robbed you of your words? Does that feeling make you feel powerless or angry? How often have you tried to tell someone what you want, but just could not find the right words? Did you just stuff your thoughts and feelings until you could not take it any longer while your body finally exploded with all those stored feelings and emotions that you kept inside for such a long time?

What if you feel you are a good communicator but, no one seems to listen to you any more? What happened to the power of your words? What about that seemingly innocent word someone used that triggered an emotional response in you – how did they know that was a sensitive issue for you? You also may not have realized that you were sensitive to an issue until a comment spoken by another person caused something to erupt inside you. However, now that those words have been spoken, you are identifying all the little things that caused you hurt and anger. How interesting it is to explore how much words impact our daily lives without us realizing the impact those words have on our psyche.

Oh, we could all go on and on about how someone's words affected us; if we thought a bit longer we could dream about how our words, appropriately constructed, might have had a more powerful impact on others!

I spent many years just watching, listening and wondering why words seemed to be the basis of all actions, emotions and thoughts, and that is why I wrote this book. The goal of this book is to help people understand how our words have overt or implied outcomes that affect the actions and behaviors of others. Using InterActive speech is a means of tweaking your current speech patterns to help you or others gain internal control of one's actions, renew respect and resolve differences without fighting and aggressiveness. This impact can start as young as infancy and proceed until the moment of death.

Those who are proficient at using their words fare well. But, how do we get to that place where we can use our words in ways that are effective for us and those around us? I've pondered this question for years, and after much thought, review of theory and experience, I devised six easy steps to help us become the owner of our lives.

The Six Steps

The six basic steps are as follows:

- **Set boundaries**
- **Ask, don't tell**
- **Use empathy**
- **Don't judge – just listen**
- **Use extension words**
- **Use the last word or concept**

Each step will be explained and examples used to help you understand how each step plays out in our daily lives. **Note you don't have to use all steps in each conversation.** Sometimes you may use just one step and other times you may end up using all steps to attain your social/ conversational goals.

Step #1 Setting Boundaries or Parameters

I have designed the first step as the foundation for any expectation we want to derive from others. If we don't know what is expected of us, we don't know how to react or what to do when we are told we are not acting or communicating appropriately. In any situation, we need to know our boundaries so we are able to interact more comfortably.

Therefore, the first step involves setting boundaries. This means we should discuss, teach, or demonstrate what we desire or expect from the other person. For example, if we are going to ask a person to keep his/her desk clean, we need to determine what the word "clean" means to each of us. I might consider "clean" as having all papers and other items neatly placed on the desk. However, the other person may interpret "clean" as washing the desk down daily! Therefore, if I came into the office the day after our initial discussion related to having a "clean" desk and the other person used his or her own interpretation of that word, we may end up having an argument about not attending to our previous discussion on maintaining a "clean" desk.

The argument could be avoided by simply clarifying "clean" so that both parties are comfortable with the common goal. This may sound very simplistic but if you look at the little "tiffs" we get into daily, you may now have the opportunity to see how easily they could have been avoided if we had set appropriate boundaries or parameters.

The secondary effects of these noncompliant situations are often lengthy discussions related to how inefficient or inappropriate the noncompliant person was by not attending to the task. When we talk too much, we do not permit the person we are trying to change or instruct to make any of their own learning connections. The person who is doing all the talking is doing all the work of figuring out the problem, determining right from wrong and determining the extent to which a behavior or action is appropriate or wrong. **The listener is not doing any work nor is he/she taking any responsibility for the actions. The best way to set boundaries is to have whoever is involved with the issue talk about it with you and collectively come up with a good solution to the problem.** Once the boundaries or rules are composed, you can then expect all involved to comply with those parameters. Here is how to do it.

1. **Define what you specifically want done**. For example, if you want the child to start her homework as soon as she comes home, you discuss this with your child and she says that she wants time to just relax after school. So, you both come to the conclusion that a 30-minute break after she arrives home from school would be acceptable to both of you. (Note, I chose this topic because it tends to be the most discussed by parents and teachers.)

2. **Set the expectation for this task** Most people do not like to be told what to do so; just telling a child or young adult to do homework is often seen as a parent's ploy to control the child. However, when you both talked about what needed to be done (homework) and both of you were able to decide on a good time to relax and start work, the expectations for the task have been defined by both of you and are easier to accept because each person has had an opportunity to contribute thoughts on study start-time. To make sure that these comments are not forgotten, it is usually good to write them down so each side is comfortable when the desire to work is soon forgotten. In case this happens, you may need to revisit why it is so important to get work done soon after the person gets home from school, the following interaction may be helpful:

Mom: Why do you think I asked you to get your work done soon after you return from school?

Child: Because you told me to.

Mom: I thought we took time to discuss this point, but if you want more clarification, what benefit would you find from getting your work done early in the afternoon?

Child: I guess I won't have to spend all evening doing homework.

Mom: Good thinking! Also, you won't have to spend the evening fighting with me!

Child: Thank Goodness!

3. **Compliance through documentation** is the best and easiest way to make sure that the discussion is tethered and not broken by forgotten promises or by distractions. If you have ever worked with teenagers or even co-workers at the office, you will find that these boundaries are often stretched or forgotten shortly after they are made. Why? Because nothing was written down to document the pact. Therefore,

when this information is not written down, no one is accountable for the discussion. If there is no documentation – there is no commitment. Now, let's complete the aforementioned conversation:

Mom: Let's make it easy on both of us by writing your homework goal on the board so we can both remember what we discussed.

Child: That way, when you want me to get to work as soon as I get home, I can show you that I have 30 minutes to watch TV or do anything I like.

Mom: True, you make a good point.

What if.....

After this initial discussion of setting boundaries, business personnel, couples, parents, educators, or anyone setting the boundaries will often ask, "What if they don't comply?" Let's say that the system only works for one day and then you are back to getting into fights again. What do you do? Go on to step #2.

Step #2 Ask, Don't Tell

Why don't people listen to us when we talk to them? Why do we have to endlessly keep telling them what to do? Why must we feel that we are losing control and respect? If you took a closer look at who is doing all the talking and who is doing all the listening, you will probably notice that the speaker, though well intentioned, is actually robbing the listener of her words. In doing so, the listener either turns off or feels the speaker is treating her like a child. Both situations often result in frustrating and angry confrontations because each party feels like their words have lost power. This concept is best exemplified by the following story.

Military Dad Story

A father came into the office to discuss problems he was having with his child. We noted that the child had a great vocabulary for his age and was able to express himself well on matters pertaining to academic subjects. Given this impressive academic knowledge, one would expect the child to be able to use those skills to monitor his own behavior and/or manage social situations. These areas, however, seemed to be very difficult for the child. We then decided to probe why this was happening. The father noted that when he spoke to his son, he tended to give directions as well as constantly explain concepts, problems and solutions needed to succeed in life.

When asked why the father talked so much to his child he noted that he was brought up with a military father who tended to dictate to his children and that was the only role-model that this father had to help him address his personal issues with his own son. We discussed possible strategies to help his son solve his own problems and come to his own solutions. First of all, I suggested using more questions rather than simply telling his son what he should do. The conversation that follows is an example of how Dr. O taught the dad how to use the Ask, Don't Tell strategy:

Dad: I tend to tell my kids what to do because it saves time and I feel that they need to know specifically what needs to be done as well as how to do it.

Dr. O: You can continue to tell your children what do to, but after you have set down your goals and expectations of what to do in a certain situation, the next step is asking them questions rather than giving them the answers.

Dad: That is going to take too much time and I can't spend my time thinking before I speak – especially when I am angry.

Dr. O: Good point. Let's talk about how the brain learns. This information will help you gain deeper insights into how a person's own language helps his or her brain develop.

I went to the white board and drew a cell, which looked like a balloon with a long tail on it and a <u>few</u> cobweb-like structures growing from that long tail. Beside that picture, I drew another balloon-like figure with <u>many</u> cobweb-like structures growing from that structure. Then I told them the following story that I read in Robert Sylwester's book. A *celebration of neurons: An educator's guide to the human brain (ASCD 1995, p. 128).*

Sylwester discusses Marion Diamond's (1988) work on brain development. Rats were used in the study because they found them to resemble those of the human brain. He noted the following:

> The basic research design (with variations) compares the brains of rats that have lived in different environments for differing periods of time: (1) rats living alone in a small, unfurnished cage, (2) a group of 12 to 36 rats living together in a large laboratory cage that contains a regularly changed and stimulating collection of toys and other objects to explore, and (3) a group of rats living in a much larger outdoor, seimnatural rat habitat. Most of the research has focused on conditions 1 and 2.

As one may expect, the researchers found that the best cortex development emerged from the social and environmental stimulation of the rat's natural habitat, followed by the enriched social cage, followed at a significantly lower level by the impoverished solitary environment.

The socially oriented seminatural and enriched laboratory settings produce a thicker and heavier cortex: larger neurons, more and better interneural connections, and a greater supply of glial support cells. These elements create a potentially better brain for learning and remembering, defined in rats by their ability to run mazes. (128)

As noted from Sylwester's example of brain development, human brains are social and in need of opportunities to solve problems, more specifically, their own problems. Given this opportunity throughout the day and continued over the years, children can then grow up to use their daily "thinking" opportunities to solve their own problems. They can come up with diverse ways to look at situations that, if they had never had the opportunity to work through at the moment of happening, would result in a textbook-type situation. Most of us have experienced these textbook situations where the teacher tells us about a topic. We take notes based on his or her words and study that information for a test. After the test, we usually have no memory of what we studied one week after we learned it. This happens because we never talked about the information or made it ours; therefore, our brain forgot it because it was not deemed important.

The military father learned from our discussion and he stopped talking to his son and listened to what his son responded when he questioned him. By doing so, he provided his son with opportunities throughout the day to use his own brain to solve problems and discuss his findings. Over time, the father did not have to keep repeating himself because his son was now able to use his own words and thought processes to figure out what needed to be done.

The military man began to understand the importance of helping his child develop his own brain through conversation rather than by giving commands and expecting conformity. When the military man did all the talking, he was developing his own brain; however, when he permitted his son to think through his own problems, the child was then able to develop his own brain.

Remember when the parent and child decided the child was permitted 30 minutes to relax after coming home from school? What will happen if the child gets distracted and forgets that he/she agreed to start schoolwork 30 minutes after coming home from school? All the parent has to do is point to the board and ask: "What do you need to be doing right now?" The child just needs to look at the board and that should be enough to get the process moving again.

Let's say the child says they feel the original idea was stupid and they no longer wanted to respect the goal. Then, I find the word "choice" an interesting way to get them moving. Just say, "OK, you are making a choice and I will respect that. However, when your favorite program comes on tonight, I will make a choice to turn it off. Do you want that to happen?"

Most often, kids will get mad and return to their original goal because it was made by both parent and child and not solely by the parent. By asking the child if the new choice is one that they don't want to respect, then the parent can provide a parent's choice to cancel something the child really enjoys.

Usually, we have found that, by asking rather than constantly telling your child, employee, and peer or loved one to do something, you are permitting them to become active participants in their own lives. Setting the parameter together and following through with that goal permit both parties to respect the goals both had set. That means that the person setting the goals also agrees to permit the employee, peer, loved one, or child to have her own personal time and that time will not be filled with other chores that the other might try to fit into that 30-minute free time. This provides stability and comfort because the person knows what is expected and how it is to be carried out. This action and respect for the boundaries set are important factors in building trust, respect and compliance.

Step #3 Empathy

Have you ever noticed how difficult it is for you to think or process information when you are upset or nervous? Have you noticed how much easier it is to accept criticism if the person presenting that critique of your work or actions sees the process from your perspective first? I call this empathy and find that all people, regardless of age or gender, respond more effectively when they know that the person critiquing their actions or work is really looking at them as a person and not as a something that needs to be fixed or changed. The latter has the potential of producing a threat.

Why use empathy? Eric Jensen describes what happens in the brain when we feel threatened. Jensen explains:

> Learning happens in many complex layers. Retrieval of some learning seems to require specific physiological states, suggesting the role of emotions in memory. In fact, emotion turns out to be one of the most important regulators of learning and memory. . . Negative emotional events, as you might expect, weigh heavily on the brain. They seem to "drag down" more of the brain's other circuits (Ito, Larsen, Smith, & Cacioppo, 2001). We recall negative emotional events longer, and they affect more brain circuits. (pp. 55-56). [Jensen, Eric (2005). *Teaching with the brain in mind – 2nd ed.* Alexandria, VA, Association for Supervision and Curriculum Development.]

After finding out how much of an impact emotional slaps have on a person's delicate system, we can now understand why it is so important to include empathy when talking with them about sensitive issues. Hence, the process I recommend in using empathy is to be sensitive to all factors involved in the situation you want to discuss. This step is especially powerful when you need to discuss an issue that may possibly cause the receiver of your words to become defensive or hurt.

Steps for Expressing Empathy

1. Define in your mind what needs to be said to that person before you start talking. Think about how you would feel if you had to receive those words. This will help you get a perspective of how you would like to receive criticism. For example: Your husband keeps interrupting you when you speak; you define:

    a. What you want to accomplish in your head – I want my husband to stop interrupting my conversations.

    b. What you want him to understand that when he takes away your words. For example, "It makes me feel like my words have no meaning and your words are more important than mine when you interrupt me during a conversation with someone else."

2. Define emotional "buzz" words such as: "interrupts" – you define that as "breaking" into YOUR conversation and, "taking over" means that he has robbed you of the opportunity to express YOUR OWN thoughts. By defining what specifically happens and how you personally define that action helps you get a good handle on what specifically upsets you and why. Many people get into "nebulous" fights because of the general comments that can't be defined or explained. For example: "You always talk when I talk." What does always mean? What does "talk when I talk" mean? – Does it mean that you talk simultaneously, that is, we are both talking at the same time? These are statements that have no defined parameter or specific example. Therefore, your words ultimately go by the wayside and you rarely resolve the issue because no one

really knows what the problem is and more specifically, how it affects YOU.

3. When dealing with a person who has difficulty accepting criticism, start your discussion by using empathy. For example, "Jim, I know you feel your comments will add to the content of this conversation and I will appreciate your input when I have completed my thoughts." This subtle comment gives the person who is interrupting you a cue to wait until you have completed your thoughts before he or she provides their own point of view. Your empathy needs to be explicit and defined so the person who interrupts you will understand how you feel and what he or she needs to do to address the issue.

4. Be explicit with defining the issue that is bothering you and that is having an emotional impact on you. For example you have previously defined two specific issues: 1) interrupting your conversation and; 2) taking over your words. Now you can help Jim understand that, when you were talking with Jack, he interrupted your conversational flow. This made you feel like he was robbing you of the opportunity to express yourself. When that happens, you feel that he is taking over your words because your words are not as important as his. When he continues to do that during many of your conversations with Jack and other friends, you wonder if he thinks that you are not as adequate as he is or if he is doing the talking for you, as a means of protecting you. This undefined perception leads us to the next step, "Listen, and don't judge."

Step #4 Listen, and Don't Judge

How many of us actually listen to what other people say – especially when we feel hurt and upset? Listening without providing judgment is most difficult when you feel you have been hurt or put down. Therefore, we need to first acknowledge what we are doing before we take verbal or physical action.

Let's revisit the prior situation where Jim kept taking over the conversations and see how this scenario could play out.

Jim: I wasn't aware that I was interrupting your conversations with Jack. Why didn't you tell me about this sooner?

You: I thought you did it on purpose to put me down.

Jim: Why would I want to purposely put you down?

You: I don't know – is it because you feel that I'm not as intelligent as you and that your words are more important than mine?

Jim: Gee, I never realized that I was implying that but, now that you mention it, I feel that sometimes you talk about our private life and that makes me feel uncomfortable.

You: Wow! I thought that Jack was your best friend and he already knew all about our personal life.

Jim: No, guys are not like girls and we don't spend our time talking about the personal stuff like that. So, when you talk about us, I feel like I need to protect our privacy.

You: Why didn't you tell me sooner?

Jim: I was afraid you'd just take it the wrong way and we'd end up in a fight.

You: Well, I still feel you are taking over the conversation to make me feel inferior and the reason I say that's because you tend to do it each time I talk with Jack.

Jim: I never wanted you to feel inferior. I guess I was just trying to protect my ego and didn't want you to tell personal things about me to other people. Why not give me a sign when you see me taking over the conversation so that I can be more aware of it next time.

You: That will be a good opportunity for me to see if you're trying to make me feel inferior or if we're just misreading each other's actions. Next time you start to take over the conversation, I'll give you a verbal cue. When you hear it, will you respect my concerns?

Jim: Sure, if this is a bad habit – I'll be able to use this cue to help me be more aware each time it happens. Now, if I didn't respect you, would I be asking you for your help?

You: Maybe I was being too sensitive. I'll try to understand your perspective and not talk about our personal issues in front of Jack.

Although this scenario may seem like a trivial piece in this whole perspective of language interactions, it is actually a mountain when it comes to feeling appreciated, valued and respected. Now let's talk about steps to listening before judging.

Listening Before Judging Techniques

Notice how easily the aforementioned scenario flowed once the specific problems were defined. The two major points – interrupting your conversation and taking over your words helped each person know what was going on and how you felt when that happened. Next, the conversation evolved to open up a new perspective on why that always happened in conversations with Jack. When we **really** listen to what the other person says without prior judgment of what that person will say, the real truth comes out. I don't think either party suspected the real reason for the conversational interruptions; once the discussion of listening without judging took place, the truth was able to come out and the underlying issues were now placed on the table. Once they are spoken, even though you may not like what you hear, you will now be able to address these issues and resolve the underlying conflicts. Before you both meet with Jack again, you can talk about the issues and come up with a way for each of you to know that the other person is overstepping boundaries. For example, you may want to agree on a verbal or visual cue when Jim interrupts you:

You: [verbal cue to Jim] Jim, am I still talking?

Jim: [understands the verbal cue] Right.

You: Last night... [You start talking again and notice Jim is looking at you as if to warn you not to talk about your personal life]

Jim: [Looks at you and makes eye contact]

You: [You smile at Jim to give him the cue that you understood his look] Last night we went to that new restaurant you recommended and it was great!

Jim: [Jim returns the smile] Yeah, thanks for the recommendation. Let's go there again when my sister comes to town.

Note that, although both were on the edge because each was trying the new techniques that were different from those they had been using, being patient and LISTENING before reacting helped the conversation continue without problems. Obviously, both parties will need to be more sensitive to the way they converse in the future, until they break the habit of either breaking into the conversation or speaking about personal relationship items. Overall, the act of listening before judging permits the real issues and problems to emerge without fighting.

If we want to succeed with our peers, family members and anyone else, just remember, we need to recognize the feelings of others when we enter into conversations with them. People who are considerate of another's personal feelings when conversing are considered caring, warm and naturally good leaders. Who would have thought that something so minuscule as taking another person's feelings or actions into consideration before we make a statement can be so powerful?

Now, let's talk about the long-term effect of how lack of sensitivity to the words we use can cause severe emotional reactions that can have a powerful impact on another's life. I call these situational comments "Demon words" because they often infiltrate our very being in ways that are subtle, strong, and so debilitating that they can actually ruin a person for a lifetime.

Answers = Assessment

People often feel that giving up the power of speech results in permitting the person with whom we speak to take control of the situation. However, if you actually listen to the reply given to your question, you might be quite surprised with the response you get.

One day, a couple came into the office to discuss some problems they were having. The husband was somewhat aggressive and quickly took over the conversation if his wife said something that he did not like.

In a prior session, his wife noted that she was diagnosed with learning problems when she was young and grew up believing that she was not very bright. Their son was having problems in school and the mother wanted to home school him rather than send him to school.

After much thought, the father noted: I don't think we are prepared to home-school our son. [His wife assessed that comment to mean she was not intellectually competent and she was not able to home-school their son.]

Wife: Oh, you think I'm too dumb to work with him at home!

Husband: I did NOT say you were dumb! I just feel that neither you nor I can even help him with his Mathematics or English while he is currently in school. How are we going to take on the responsibility to teach him these subjects at home?

Wife: You know I was diagnosed with a learning problem when I was in school and I have always been sensitive about people thinking I was not very smart. Therefore, when you told Dr. O that "we" were not prepared to teach our son at home, I took your comment as a personal insult that you didn't have confidence in my ability to teach our son at home. You know you won't have time to work with him at home so I'll be the responsible teacher, and now I know you don't have confidence in me.

To repair the situation I asked the husband to place himself in his wife's situation knowing that she was not comfortable with the way she was treated as a child. Then we replayed the scenario using the comments made as a means of assessing how to proceed with the conversation.

Husband: I don't feel we are prepared to teach our son at home.

Wife: Oh, you think I'm too dumb!

Husband: What words did I use to make you feel dumb?

Wife: You said, "We weren't prepared to teach our child at home!"

Husband: True, do we currently have problems helping him with his Mathematics and English?

Wife: Yes. There are evenings when neither of us can help him with his homework.

Husband: So, if I also have difficulty teaching our son, why would you personalize that comment?

Wife: I guess I let my past get in the way of my emotions.

Husband: I understand how you feel about your past and how it affects you emotionally. Now that I've provided my rationale for why we can't home-school our son, do you feel more comfortable with that decision?

Wife: Now that you've put it that way, I understand why you made the comment and I must agree with your rationale.

The husband and wife were glad they were able to repair their misconceptions but wondered how they could continue this process alone and without my assistance. I wrote the following steps:

Steps for Improving Communication

1. Start with what you observed. For example: I noted that when you said, "We're not prepared to teach our son at home," you were actually being honest noting the difficulty of his current coursework.

    a. When the husband made that statement, he did not consider how sensitive his wife was regarding her negative past learning experiences.

    b. His wife observed his reluctance to permitting home-schooling and took that comment as a personal slight on her.

    c. Both adults misread the comments made by the other and did not go a step farther to assess the impact their words had on the other person.

2. To improve the conversation after these words were spoken, determine how you want to use referent words in the future. Go back to the scenario and start from where the conversation started to get difficult and revisit those comments. The hard part here is to try to keep an open mind when listening to the comments made by the other person.

3. After you hear what the other person says, assess what those comments mean to the person who made them.

4. If the wife assessed her husband's comments regarding the fact that they were not prepared to teach their son, she could have asked for a clarification of what he meant by that statement. That way, she would have been able to understand that

the material at their son's grade level was beyond their current knowledge base.

5. When the husband heard his wife's comment about being dumb, he could use that knowledge as a means of knowing how sensitive she would be to any future comments regarding her own intelligence.

In essence, we can all learn from every conversation with others by listening to the comments, assessing what has been said and determining how to proceed with the conversation so that all entities are comfortable.

Resolving a Prior Verbal Exchange or Conflict

We often want to bring up unresolved situations so we can either get in the final word or just get a better understanding of what really happened to cause an uncomfortable situation or fight. The way we handled that situation can either bring resolution to the topic or conjure up anger and more disdain.

The following is an example of resolving a prior conflict. A couple was going out for the evening and the husband told his wife he loved her. He was shocked when she replied, "No you don't!" Well, let's revisit it and try to resolve what really set the wife off that evening.

Husband: Honey, remember when we went to the movies last week and you made a comment that "I did not love you"? Well, I would like to revisit that situation without us fighting this time. I know you had strong feelings when you made that comment and I want to see what I may have done to cause you to feel unloved.

Wife: Well, you never take me to the movies I want to go to and we always have to go to the war movies and stuff you like or we never go to the movies.

Husband: [starting with empathy] I guess it never occurred to me that you didn't like the same kinds of movies I like.

Wife: That's true. You know I always say those movies you choose are violent.

Husband: Yes, you say they are violent. But you still go and don't give me any other choices of movies you want to see. So, I just thought that you were fine with the choices I made.

Wife: Well, now you know I don't like them.

Husband: Yes, now I know you don't like them and now you know that you have the right to give me other choices so we can both enjoy our evening out together.

Husband: Now, is it still true that you feel I don't love you?

Wife: Now that I know you understand how I feel about violent movies and that you are willing to consider a movie we both would enjoy – I guess it shows that you really do care for me.

Husband: Maybe we should change that word care to LOVE. I really do love you – in the future, please don't use such harsh words regarding how I feel about you. It gives me mixed messages about how you really do feel about me. Do you love me?

Wife: Of course I do silly. I just wanted to make my point.

Husband: OK point made – topic resolved ---- Right?

Wife: Yes! [Wife laughs]

Now, you are probably thinking that each of these scenarios has a happy ending, but you can open a topic and realize that it is not the time to resolve it because there is still tension in the air and one or both of you are not ready to use your words to discuss a previous situation. Imagine if the previous scenario evolved in a different way.

Husband: So the situation is resolved – right. [The husband looks directly at his wife to ascertain her reaction to his comment.]

Wife: No, that is just one topic that makes me mad. There are many things I don't like about you and I've had a bad day so don't talk to me right now. [The wife does not look at her husband when she talks to him.]

Husband: Is the bad mood related to something else I've done or is it something you need to resolve yourself? [The husband looks at his wife with concern in his eyes.]

Wife: I'm about to get my period and am just not feeling well. So maybe we should talk when I'm in a better frame of mind. [The wife feels his concern and looks at him to make sure he understands her comment.]

Husband: Good point – we can resolve this later. I'm going out to pick up the kids from baseball. [He makes eye contact with her then walks away to give her time to herself.]

By giving a person permission to have a bad day tends to defuse a probably combustible situation. Listening to the rationale for their bad mood may also add insights we would not have been able to glean from a heated argument.

Believe it or not, the action of understanding another person's need for quiet or solitude is a form of empathy. A subtle, but highly effective nuance to use during these difficult situations is eye contact. Eye contact in the last situation is very important because looking into another person's eyes is like looking into their heart. Your sincerity will be felt in both the words you use as well as the look you give that person when you say those words.

Misinterpretations of meaning and sincerity are stronger when you come face to face with a person. When we talk to a person's back or listen to another person with our back turned to them, we are giving them the nonverbal body position that they are not important. Even though we may use empathy, those comments will have little or no impact if we don't connect directly with the one receiving our words.

Step #5 Extending Speech

What do you do with the non-conversant person? I often have people complain that they want to talk with the person with whom they are in conflict, but that person always clams up and won't talk. To resolve this point, I usually recommend "extended speech" as a means of using connecting words such as: and....so....because.....also.....etc. as a means to encourage the nonverbal person to engage in further discussion or explanation of a topic.

The classic conversation stopper is the closed ended question.

How was_____ [school, work, mom, etc.]?

We usually get the reply: good [and the conversation ends there]

If we really want to get into a conversation with a non-conversant person, we might want to use extended speech. Let's look at an example.

Jack comes home from work and seems to be in a bad mood. Sally feels that he is angry and begins to think it might be directed at her but she does not know how to get that out of him.

Sally: Hey Jack!

Jack: Hey.

Sally: How was your day?

Jack: Fine [sits down on the couch with a beer and turns on the TV while ignoring Sally]

Sally: Are you mad at me?

Jack: No

Sally feels frustrated but does not know how to continue the conversation. So she goes to her room and sulks for the rest of the evening. They go to bed without talking to each other and this cold treatment may go on for days without either of them really knowing what was wrong or how to repair the damage. Let's try this scenario again:

Sally: Hey Jack!

Jack: Hey.

Sally: How was your day?

Jack: Fine.

Sally: How nice, because?

Jack: Because it was not so bad.

Sally: And "not so bad means....?"

Jack: It means it could have been better.

Sally: and...

Jack: And, if it were better, I would've had the guts to tell my boss off.

Sally: when...

Jack: When he told me to shut up during our group meeting today.

Sally: and...

Jack: And, I didn't want to make a fool of myself so I just sat down and shut up but I feel he needs to hear what I was trying to explain because it would really help the project.

Sally: so tomorrow you can....

Jack: Hum, I can see him privately and explain my thoughts without having him make a fool of me in public.

Sally: by saying...

Jack: I guess I could start by telling him that although his comment about me shutting up made me feel uncomfortable, I'd like to revisit the situation to help him understand my rationale for speaking up at the meeting.

Sally: therefore...

Jack: If I give my rationale, I know he'll realize that I wasn't trying to criticize his proposal but bring to light the new information I received about that company.

Jack: [looks up from the TV and at Sally saying] Gee Sally, I appreciate your help! You made some good points and helped me think how I want to approach my boss tomorrow. [He leans over and gives her a kiss and Sally just smiles to herself].

After you read this scenario, I am sure it conjured up in your own mind a situation where you basically said nothing – just connected words – and the other person in the conversation felt you worked wonders for their ability to work through a problem! The real helper here was the connecting words and your look of genuine concern for that person's feelings. Isn't it interesting how those two simple acts can help a person feel better with little or no work on your part?

If we look back, in the previous conversation you can see that Jack often used the connection word Sally used as a means of connecting his own thoughts. These connection words actually helped Jack continue processing difficult information so he could sort out what really happened and determine how to improve the situation the next day. This process brings us to the next step because it builds on ways we can use another person's words to build deeper information processing.

Step #6 Use the Last Word or Concept

When you want a person to know that you really are listening to what they are saying or if you want to make an impact on that person's conversational patterns, you can use the last word or concept they used as the beginning response to that person.

This process works really well with teenagers because they often complain that their parents never listen to them. Dr. Keith Ablow, a psychologist on national TV, had a group of sisters on his show discussing how their dad damaged them as kids because he treated them aggressively and often hurt their emotional feelings. When Dr. Keith tried to get these women to provide specific instances of their dad's abuse, none of them could provide a specific scenario. These women felt disrespected when their dad ignored their words and their need for an appropriate response to their comments. To make sure this does not happen in your own relationships, you might want to read the following two scenarios.

The Wrong Order

A businessman came into my office the other day and said, "I had a situation this week that reminded me of the way you talk." He told me that his company made a mistake on a purchase a contractor made. The contractor was upset at the mistakes; therefore, the salesman took a cue from him and started raising his voice and getting very angry and upset with the main office purchasing department. The contractor was on the other phone in his office listening to the conversation. When he calmed himself down and started asking questions related to the purchasing director's comments. The questions flowed based on the last thing that came out of the purchase director's mouth. In essence, the contractor was listening to the last words or concepts the director made and used those words or comments to start his next question. The conversation lasted two hours! The end result was a remedied situation without anger, frustration or misunderstandings.

I asked the businessman how he felt about the way the contractor had handled himself and the situation. He said the man's questioning made him look like he was in control the whole time and he gained respect and understanding from all who worked with him. He said it was a very powerful situation and vowed to try to continue using it on a regular basis. I noted that when people start using this technique they never return to their old style of aggression, anger and frustration because you can walk away from any difficult situation when using InterActive speech and feel you have maintained the respect and power you deserved in the first place.

Now that you have a basic idea of how the steps are defined and used, let's look at a few case studies and see how you do at improving each scenario using InterActive speech.

Case Studies

Read through the different cases described here and note how those petty instances that play out throughout our days add up to making our daily lives comfortable or pure hell. The scenarios are reviewed in Appendix A so you can compare how you would handle each situation with how it would be handled using InterActive speech.

The Boss Story

Mr. Richards is a pretty nice guy. He dresses well, smells good, and always has a smile on his face, but why don't his employees like him? Well, I just overheard him talking with Mary, an employee who has been with him for the last 15 years, and the conversation went like this:

Mary: Get me the Gibson file – he says as he rushes in front of her desk.

Mary brings the file and asks: Do you want me to call Mr. Gibson for you?

Mr. Richards: What do you think I'm dumb or something? I have fingers and can call him when I'm ready.

Mary: I just wanted to see if you needed some help.

Mr. Richards: If I wanted a mother, I'd have my mother working in your place.

Mary feels like she is being put down by Mr. Richards all the time and Mr. Richards feels like Mary is always trying to meddle in his life. Over the years, the words have become a harbor of thoughts without a boat to guide them to shore. The result is two people who have a love/hate relationship because they have learned to live with each other. They need each other but their days are filled with pain and frustration.

The Word-Robbing Family

One day a Teenager entered my office, quickly plopped down and slouched into the corner of the long couch. Although there was plenty of room on the couch, her mother sat on a chair across from her. The father grabbed a chair from behind my desk. Her father started talking about his daughter's problems in school. Each time the daughter tried to tell her side of the story, the father told her to wait until he was finished with his comments. That comment made the young lady pull her coat even closer to her chest and hold her arms tightly around herself. Mom's eyes kept moving from her daughter to her husband trying to determine how to intervene. Finally, the father stopped discussing how he viewed his daughter's problems, and his daughter tried to provide her side of the story. About half-way through her interpretation of her academic issues, her mother stepped in to add her comments. As soon as mother took over, the child went back to cuddling her coat and looking down at the floor. No eye contact was made among any of the family members until dad took over the conversation from the mother. The mother gave a cold look at him, which he ignored, and continued speaking. This round-robin of lost words continued for about fifteen minutes. By the time I stopped the never-ending rally of unending sentences, all family members were holding their folded arms closely to their chests.

What would you do to help this family? What was the main problem in this scenario and how would you help the family without pointing fingers and getting them more fired up than they are right now? Would you do anything to help the daughter?

The Stepparents

Jean and John were very much in love and both had children from their previous marriages. When they married, they thought it would be great to bring up a "Brady Bunch." However, the two of them each had a different way of bringing up their children and neither knew the extent of the personal history the children had experienced before both of them got together. Therefore, when they tried to discipline the children, each child would run to their birth parent for advice and counsel. They also felt they were not understood by the new parent because each parent used words and comments that made them feel uncomfortable. In essence, there is no common language or rules that made them feel like a family. How did the Brady Bunch learn to live together or maybe we should explore how they talked to each other?

The Friends

Mary, Max, Ed, and Jane have been friends from birth. They went to the same schools and continue to keep in touch with each other. As they grow, so do their experiences. However, every once in a while, someone will talk about a confidential situation that proves embarrassing; this situation is rarely resolved because someone usually ends up getting hurt and walking away. What words can you use to put the person in their place and still remain friends without fighting? How can this group let each other know they are overstepping boundaries without getting into fights?

The Couple

Jen and Jack have been married for five years. Jen feels that Jack has grown too comfortable with their relationship. He forgets to do nice things for her and expects to come home and have sex whenever he gets in the mood. Jen wants to tell him about her needs but knows that they will end up in a fight with both shutting down. So, rather than fight, both parties go through life angry with each other. Now they are beginning to question their love for each other and are contemplating divorce. How can they start to use their words to bring themselves back together and rekindle the fire they once had? How can they discuss sensitive wants and needs without the other person walking away?

The Boy Scouts

The big overnight weekend had arrived and all the boys took turns working toward their badges. The scout leader noticed tension with one of the boys (John). Before he could go up to ask what was wrong, he caught John punching Jim in the face. Upon further examination, he found out that the other scouts were picking on John. Finally, John could not take it any longer and just exploded. The scout leader took the two boys aside and told them how to behave at camp. He explained how their actions were inappropriate and told them they needed to learn how to interact without hitting or punching. He talked with the rest of the boys in the group and told them not to bully others and to respect each other. After the discussion, the boys went on their way leaving John by himself for fear of either getting into trouble or getting hit by him.

How would you have handled this situation? Do you think the boys understood the problem and were able to improve their behaviors?

Now that you have read the case studies, let's perfect your InterActive speech process by shedding light on some nuances of interpersonal interactions. Sometimes just using these hints can help you accomplish your goals. When used in conjunction with some or all of the six steps, they add impact to your conversations.

Nuances that Make a Difference

When we talk we also use our bodies to help us add emphasis to our intentions. If we astutely listen to another person speak, we can often determine how that person processes information. For example, visual people tend to say, "Yea, I see, I see" when we explain something to them because they are accustomed to viewing the situation by using their eyes. Auditory learners tend to use phrases like, "I hear you, yea – that sounds great." These people tend to be better at listening to what you say than being shown with their eyes. Have you ever tried to give directions to someone who likes to process information with their eyes? They will usually tell you to draw them a map. A person who likes to use their ears to process information might say – "that's too much stuff on the paper; just tell me how to get there."

Although these are subtitle conversational nuances, people get into trouble when their modes of processing information differ. Classrooms or office meetings are perfect examples of how people react to differing processing styles. If a visual person gets overwhelmed with too much talking, he may open his book or manual to find a picture to lead him through the words being spoken. A person who processes through his ears might get visually overwhelmed with too many slides or too many words written on them. The auditory learner may even put his head down or look like he is not listening, but he is looking away because the overabundance of visuals is causing him to shut down. This nuance alone would help speakers, teachers, and administrators to diversify their presentations in order to attend to all people in the audience. The next nuance group tends to see the world from the "big picture" or from "small pieces."

Generalists and Specifists

Another little-known concept to how people process information tends to break down into two groups "Generalists" or "Specialists." I call them "Generalist and Specialists" because the former group tends to see the world as a whole or the big picture. The latter group sees the pieces and may have difficulty pulling those pieces together to get the whole concept. Although we all vacillate from one style to another throughout the day, we tend to gravitate to one style more than the other.

When two similar styles are together they relish the conversational nuances because the words such as "**always**" and "**never**" are accepted verbiage for the "Generalists." "Specialists," on the other hand, relish in details! They really enjoy knowing specific dates, time, places, and all the specific details of a story.

When two opposing styles get together, however, the "Generalist" terms are defined as an action or event that takes place on a regular basis by the "Specialist". That is fine on a positive note such as, "You <u>always</u> buy me flowers!" [When, he only brought them on one other occasion]. On a negative note, however, when the "Specialist" is blamed such as, "You <u>never</u> take me out to dinner," [When they go out at least once a week]. You can see how the "Specialist" feels slighted and unappreciated.

The same holds true for the "Specialist" when confronted with a "Generalist". The terms such as "always" and "never" does not provide enough evidence to substantiate the claims. When a "Specialist" asks for specific proof from a "Generalist", they are often considered nick picky. Also, when a "Specialist" asks for specific proof from a "Generalist", they are often considered nick picky and overbearing.

A good example of how a "Generalist" thinks is shown by how my husband and I view the lint that collects on the dryer screen. One day he went to remove the clothes from the dryer and yelled, "Dianne, you ALWAYS leave lint on the dryer screen!"

I thought for a second and asked, "Were the clothes still in the dryer?"

My husband: Yes

Me: I find it hard to remove dryer lint when the clothes are still in the process of drying. So, that may be why you feel I ALWAYS forget to empty the lint screen!

As you can see my husband only noted the big picture – lint on the dryer screen. He did not take into consideration one detail – drying clothes make lint, which cannot be removed until the clothes are dried. The fact that he used the word "always" could have been grounds for an argument had I not figured out that he is a "Generalist" and his comment should not be taken to heart but rather used as an observation that needed clarification.

Now, a person on the opposite side of the spectrum is usually the very detailed person who sees and remembers too many details. Those people drive "Generalists" crazy because when they fight, they tend to cite specific instances where the offender was wrong. Since many generalists tend to forget what they do from one minute to another, the generalist cannot even refute the wrong because they forgot the situation soon after it happened.

The Husband and Wife Springtime Story

A husband and wife were driving down Main Street on a summer afternoon. The "Specialist" husband remarked that many of the women were already wearing summer clothing. The "Generalist" wife felt that he was looking at the women and took his remark to imply that he was a womanizer who could not keep his eyes off other women. A big fight resulted, where she accused him of ALWAYS looking at women. However, from his mindset, he only meant to make a remark about a specific thing he noticed about the way the women were dressed.

When "Generalist" and "Specialist" couples come into my office, I try to point out the major differences in the way they seem to be wired, and ask that they take that into consideration the next time they get into a disagreement. The next thing I recommend is that they explore the words each used in the confrontational conversation. More than likely, they will point out "Generalistic" and "Specialistic" terms that really got on each other's nerves. Next, I ask the couple to determine who is more upset or unnerved by the situation and, if it has more bearing on one partner than the other. They should recognize this and move on. The dryer lint story is a good example of how to move on when we do not want to have a fight. I just thought, "Whose problem is this?" My husband seems to be more concerned with the lint in the dryer than me, so, he will have to understand why he gets upset at the lint. Maybe I just need to help him see the specifics of the situation to help him relax next time he sees lint on the dryer screen."

Just knowing how he is wired helped me stop feeling that he was making a personal statement about my cleanliness and helped me ward off a fight. It also helped to release my tension when I noticed that the lint was more of a problem to him than it was to me. Therefore, rather than spend the rest of the day fighting, I just listened to his words and used my logical questioning to help him understand the issue.

Teenagers are often victims of the "Generalist/Specialist" difficulties because they often see the world from either the big picture or they pick up on specific details that are very important to themselves but often unimportant to others. This form of processing often results in heated battles with their parents, siblings, peers, and teachers. They get themselves so emotionally involved in other people's problems that they end up emotionally drained at the end of the day. To help ward off heated discussions and arguments, we might want to:

- First determine how the teenager is seeing that particular situation. Are they viewing it from a "Generalist's" perspective by using words such as "you ALWAYS_____" or he/she NEVER ___" etc.

- If not, determine if he/she is picking up on little details and using those details to become emotionally upset?

- If that is the case, assistance and possible diffusion of frustration might begin by determining what the "specific" problem is in the first place.

- By defining the "real" issue, you can help the teenager defuse the emotions tied to that particular situation.

- Finally, you might want to help teenagers determine if the problem really involves them or is it something their friends need to deal with. This piece helps teenagers stay out of other people's issues.

The "Generalist" Teenager Story

Jane: My friend's boyfriend NEVER attends to her needs and I think I should call him and let him know how mean he always is to her!

Jane's mom: (identifying the specific issue) What did he do to make your friend feel bad?

Jane: Well, today was the Valentine flower drive and he didn't even give her a flower! That's so rude and she felt so bad when ALL the other girls got flowers from their boyfriends!

Jane's mom: First of all, did EVERYONE really get flowers from their boyfriends, and what does he constantly do that you feel is MEAN to her?

Jane: Well, now that I think about it – lots of girls did not get flowers and I heard her tell Mary that he was going to take her out to dinner tonight.

Jane's mom: Well, could he be saving his money for a nice dinner alone with her tonight? Isn't that being nice to her?

Jane: Yeah, but I think he should let her know how much he cares for her by giving her a flower at school so EVERYONE can see how much he likes her!

Jane's mom: Hmm – is it possible that you are wondering if he REALLY likes her so maybe you could make a move on him? If she really wanted him to spend the dinner money on a flower – shouldn't she have told him that on her own?

Jane: You're right on both counts, Mom.

Jane's mom: Before you start getting involved in your friend's problems and getting yourself upset, maybe you should just ask yourself, "Whose problem is this?"

Jane: Well, I guess I'm making it my problem because I kind of like him and I'd like to really know how much he likes her. So, by his not giving her a flower at school makes me believe there's a chance for me to go out with him.

Jane's mom: Before you start making a move on him – maybe you should think of how that one action fits into the big picture of their relationship. Now, is this really your problem or are you making it your problem?

Jane: I guess I'm making too much out of this and I should let my friend solve her own problems.

Jane's mom: Sounds like a good solution to the issue. If you had stuck your nose into her situation with her boyfriend and they ended up having a fight, you may be blamed for everything, and he may not want to have you as a girlfriend because you were the person who started their problem in the first place. Maybe you should let them try to work out what you perceive is a problem, and if their relationship doesn't work out in the long run, then you can have a chance to vie for his feelings.

The "Specialist" Teenager Story

"Specialist" teenagers are at the other side of the spectrum. These people tend to over-analyze everything that comes out of the mouths of others. You might be able to identify this type of person by hearing remarks such as, "Why did you tell him that?" or "Did you see the stupid look he gave you?" Each little piece of the day is often so meaningful to the Specialist that they are exhausted by the end of the day and frustrated when the rest of the world can't see how important those issues really are in life! Therefore, to assist this type of person, you need to think small – very small. Since each detail will have equal weight, you may get so bogged down with these specific details that you can't get into the topic and end up forgetting the reason you wanted to intervene in the first place. For example: Jack and John were studying together for a test. Jack is very detailed and John can't stand him pointing out all the details.

Jack: Hey, let's get this Biology done first.

John: OK, I'll do the even review questions and you can do the odd ones.

[After the first question was completed, the boys discussed their answers]

Jack: Hey, you forgot to discuss the antlers and you didn't talk about the color of the body.

John: Look, the teacher just asked us to describe the fly; you don't have to tell that many details or you will be writing all night.

Jack: If you don't tell all the parts and discuss them you won't get full credit.

John: I hand my papers in all the time and I always get decent grades.

Jack: What do you call decent grades? Tell me what you got on the last two tests.

John: I don't know. I don't remember what I get on tests. I just know I passed and that was enough for me.

Jack: Well, how are you able to keep track of your grades in the class?

John: That's dumb. Who cares? If I get a passing grade I'm cool with it. Why are you making such an issue out of all this?

Jack: [Grabs John's shirt and gets ready to punch him] Dumb! Look who's dumb! You asshole – you can't even keep track of your grades. You're the dumb ass here!

John's dad hears the guys fighting and comes into the room to break it up.

Both boys could not see how they got into the fight and left without further discussions because John felt that Jack was being picky and too sensitive, and Jack felt that John was irresponsible and inappropriate.

Can you determine which boy was a Generalist and which one was a Specialist? Had they known their personality types, they would have been able to pick up on the nuances that got them into this confrontation. John's dad did not think about differences in personality types and could not understand what happened. The boys ended a friendship which could have been complimentary. Jack could have done all the detailed work on the review and John could have found the general information and helped Jack pull the information together to make a comprehensive essay. Now this friendship is lost. Neither guy actually knew why it ended.

Business World Generalists and Specialists

Although we tend to pick professions based on our love or hate for details, working with someone from either side of the spectrum can be difficult. The "Generalist" will want to gloss over the details and get to the bottom line in business meetings and/or negotiations. However, this type of person would drive a "Specialist" crazy because he/she needs the details to feel comfortable and know every piece of the contract or negotiation before it is set into action.

Dancing with the Stars

As I watch the program "Dancing with the Stars," I often wonder why some couples have a difficult time communicating. Obviously, the ability to learn quickly and have sufficient body capability are fundamental factors. However, underlying all the prerequisites is the fact that some people see the big picture but have difficulty translating those concepts to identifiable pieces and vice versa. I also feel that the lack of verbal communication plays a role in being able to provide information in a way that is comfortable for each person's brain to understand. Next time you watch this program or something similar, think about this point and listen for "Generalist" and "Specialist" terms and any other nuance you learn here to help you define underlying problems that may detract from success.

The aforementioned example shows how, knowing your style of processing information, would permit the dancing instructor to provide appropriate assistance to attain success in a more timely and comfortable manner.

Trigger Words

Why do some words conjure up emotions to some people and not to others? Have you ever noticed how, during a conversation with someone, your words seem to cause anger or frustration in the other person? In your mind, you think you are speaking about something very mundane, but the reaction from the other person shows you that you said something that really touched a nerve. The following scenario provides more details.

I was working with a stepfather and his stepson one evening when the conversation turned to anger and hate at the drop of a few words. I went back and asked each to examine those words to help us all get a better feel for why they had such an impact on the conversation. The story transpired as followed:

The Disrespectful Stepson Story

One day the stepson was being very disrespectful to his mother and this disrespect caused the stepfather to have emotional flashbacks to his own childhood. He did not disclose his past situation with his stepson; he just became very angry and aggressive with his stepson's disrespectful words and actions. Although the stepson realized that his stepfather was correct in making him apologize to his mother, he could not forgive him for his extremely aggressive reaction. Although nothing was brought up after that altercation, an air of tension persisted until they met in my office. I asked each one to define what transpired to make their relationship so tense and awkward. At first, everyday comments such as making the bed or helping in the kitchen were discussed. Then, the stepson noted his stepfather's excessive aggression toward him and the following conversation transpired:

Stepfather: My parents had a difficult life and I was the recipient of many of their angry fights. I was even sent to a foster home because the authorities feared for my safety. After I was allowed to return home, my mother cried with me. Her tears of sadness showed me how much she cared for me. This made me feel very strongly about the relationship between a child and his mother. I respected her for her caring. Now I watch you and your mother fight and see how you disrespect your mother in your conversations and in your actions. These interactions bring back old feelings from the past.

Stepson: Hearing about your past and why you got so upset with me for being disrespectful to my mom helps me understand your anger and aggression towards me. On the one hand, I want to understand and forget what happened. However, I feel you are doing to me what my mom and birth dad did to me as a child. They kept things from me and made me feel rejected and isolated from the family unit. When you withheld the real reason for your anger toward me, I felt rejected just as I did when my parents fought, and kept me from knowing what was happening to their marriage.

Two innocent words "disrespect" and "rejected" had different meanings to each person in the conversations. Each one could rationalize the impact it had on the other but each one also knew that the emotional underpinnings needed time to heal. Opening the door to "trigger words" provided an opportunity to continue their discussions in a more open and emotionally sensitive way. They pay closer attention to each other's body language taking time to stop and discuss if the words they are using are too harsh, or if the words are conjuring up deep emotional feelings from the past. Given their shared emotional difficulties, both men have become closer than they had been because they now are able to share stories and emotional feelings from their sad and difficult pasts.

Similar situations can play out in business, education, casual and intimate relationships. Knowing more about the impact words have on others can help us when we are in these situations.

How to spot "Trigger Words"

Since we cannot know everything about each person's past nor can we be privy to every person's emotional past life, we need to listen to the words we use and watch the body language of the person with whom we speak. You might note that the impact can have diverse effects on each person. One person may just take in the information without any emotional reaction and another person will bristle with anger and emotion.

When we are in those types of situations we can either turn our heads or not pay attention to what we have experienced; or, we can bring up what we have observed and work through it. Let's look at a scenario to help you to get a better understanding of how to work through a difficult situation.

The Stepmother's Story

A stepmother asked her stepdaughter to clean the kitchen after lunch. She went into her room and started working on the computer instead of cleaning the kitchen. When the stepmother saw what had happened, she said, "The only time we can get out of an obligation is when we die. So go to the kitchen and do the dishes!"

Within seconds, the stepdaughter was in tears and slammed the door in her stepmother's face. What could have caused the stepdaughter to overreact so strongly? When the stepmother saw this reaction, she asked the stepdaughter to open her door. She wanted to understand what was causing her to feel so angry.

Stepmother: Mary, I'm not sure why you reacted so violently to my request. Open the door and let's talk.

Mary: Leave me alone. You wouldn't understand anyway!

Stepmother: If you open the door, you can give me the chance to understand your frustration with me.

Mary: [opens the door and flings herself on the bed crying – the stepmother goes over and asks if she can just sit with her a second] I guess. I'm just frustrated right now.

Stepmother: Because…?

Mary: Because when you said, "The only time we can get out of a situation is when we die." You forgot that my dad died and I felt that you were disrespecting me and my dad when you said that.

Stepmother: Gee! That phrase is what my mom used to say to me when I was your age. She used to say it to let me know that there was no good reason for me to get out of doing my chores. Since I understood why she said it and since I did not have your same experience, I thought you would accept my comment with the same interpretation. I didn't even think about the impact those words would have on you. Forgive my insensitivity; let's try to understand each other next time by at least giving me a sign or a comment to let me know that my words are having an emotional impact on you.

Mary: I'm sorry too. I shouldn't be so aggressive with you and I need to remember that you aren't in my body so you don't know what I feel or what's happened to me in the past. I guess we just need to be more sensitive toward each other.

Stepmother: Yes, being a step-mom and a stepdaughter is not easy, but I think if we can communicate, at least we can tell each other how we feel.

The examples used in "Trigger Words" bring us to the next point, "Stuffing"

Stuffing

Most people say they hate to fight; therefore, they would rather just hold or "stuff" whatever they want to say or whatever they are thinking so that they do not have to enter into a conflict with the person with whom they are talking. Although this may get you through a situation or two, over time, anger and aggression build up inside and soon explosions result. These emotional explosions seem to come out of the blue to people receiving those actions and reactions, but it may be just the trigger words or actions that built up to such an extent that they could no longer be contained. This can be the consequence of not dealing with an issue when it happens.

The Divorcee

Prior to their divorce, Mr. and Mrs. Jones were seeing a counselor because Mr. Jones was having an affair with another woman. Over the course of two years of counseling, he swore he was not seeing that woman and told the counselor and his wife he was trying to make his marriage work. One day, his wife saw them riding past her on the highway. She was so shocked and angry with her husband for lying and **withholding** the truth that she decided to go through with the divorce. She never showed her anger toward her husband and she never told her sons why she went through with the divorce.

Embarrassed and angry, she chose to "stuff" the feelings. She felt that if she held the information long enough inside herself; it would go away and she would be able to go on with her life. She also forgot to take into consideration her children's need to know why their parents divorced. Therefore, she lived her life in silence and rarely discussed any details regarding her marriage or divorce.

Her sons were quite innocent and somewhat immature. Although they had many questions in their mind, they did not know how to voice their concerns without getting either parent angry. Their lives seemed to flow smoothly until the mother chose to make a doctor's appointment for the eldest son without discussing it with him first. Both the son and the mother were quite shocked when he came back with an angry and aggressive response to her action without discussing it with him first.

They rarely questioned her plans or her actions. Therefore, when she told her son of an appointment she had made for him, she was quite shocked at his aggressive response.

Son: Mom you keep **withholding** information from me and I just can't take it any longer.

Mom: I know you are angry with me for divorcing your dad but you don't know all the details.

Son: Mom, everything is over now and I don't even care any more about why you guys divorced.

Mom: (crying) I'm so sorry for **withholding** information from you but I never knew what was happening in your dad's life either and I really understand why you are mad at me.

Son: No Mom, you really don't get it. I hate it when you make appointments for me without even discussing it with me first.

Mom: Well, each time I ask you first, you say, "No" before I can even discuss my thoughts on why it would be good for you.

Son: Even if I tell you why I don't want to go to these dumb places, you make me go anyway. You just don't respect my wishes.

Mom: I guess I'm finally letting go of all the pent up emotions I stuffed inside for a long time. Now I'm glad at least that you are telling me what you think.

Son: I have been telling you what I think for a long time but you never listen to me. That's why I just don't say anything and I hold it all inside. Today I just could not take it any more and I had to explode. You are mad at Dad for **withholding** information from you. Have you ever realized that you are doing that same thing to us? You are **withholding** information from us and justifying it with your anger for Dad. Maybe you should learn from your experiences with Dad and start being more open with my brother and me. Then that word **withhold** won't come between us again.

The "stuffing" point here was the word, "**withhold.**" Each person had a personal emotional tie to how they were treated when information was **withheld**. Both mother and son "stuffed" their emotional response and, when it finally surfaced, it came from two different perspectives. Just listening to these two people talk made me feel like I was listening to two different conversations.

This mother-son example shows us the word "**withhold**" meant something different to each person. For the mother it meant a confidence destroyed and for the son it meant lack of confidence in his ability to make his own decisions. Bottom line on both situations was a common "trigger word" that touched deep-seated emotions.

To address these issues the mother and her son needed to define the word "**withhold**" and what it meant to each one. Then, they had to determine how they would change their behaviors so that they could have more faith in each other's decision-making process. Mom would discuss future commitments with her son before making appointments and her son would understand that she was still sensitive to the fact that his dad had withheld information from his mom who caused her pain, suffering and ultimately a divorce. This conversation was the first of many needed to repair their strained relationship.

Steps for "Trigger Word and Stuffing" Repair

1. Note the word(s) we used that caused the other person to react.

2. Try to get the other person to explain why your words caused such an emotional reaction.

3. Discuss the personal impact the words had and try not to use them in a hurtful way in the future.

4. Use future conversations to help the other person heal.

I guess the best way to deal with any of the aforementioned situations is to take a step back from the situation and think how you would feel if someone hurt your feelings. Then determine how you would want to be treated to help ease your pain. Any attempt to repair the damage by the other person would tend to be helpful and improve the relationship.

Two Trigger Word Stories

1. The first situation involves a young man who was diagnosed with attention deficit problems when he was about 7 years old. He was doing his work in class and his teacher made reference to something he produced as being "dumb." The child internalized that word as a personal reference to his own intellectual ability. Years passed and I started working with him when he was in high school. I kept hearing reference to difficult teachers as "dumb" or difficult homework as, "dumb." Hence, I questioned his referencing these people and activities with the same word. He thought for a minute and could not recall any reason to use the word except that he felt it was the best representation of his thoughts and feelings toward anyone or anything difficult. I asked him to try to bring that word to consciousness each time he used it and to pay attention to anything that came to mind. He returned a couple of weeks later with a story about a situation that took place when he was young and how the teacher's words referred to him being "dumb." Ah! Once we uncovered the basis for his demon word, we started to explore his reactions to people and tasks and discovered that he felt "dumb" when some teachers either corrected him in front of his peers or when they questioned him and he was not prepared with the correct answer. He also made reference to school tasks and determined that he considered the tasks "dumb" whenever he felt that his inability to complete them successfully would lead people to thinking he was "dumb." He never consciously realized what he had been saying

or to what reference point it was connected. However, after he realized what had happened in his life, we were able to face each situation and define his thoughts and feelings properly. Soon he realized he really was a bright person. Whenever faced with difficult tasks, he could consider them a personal challenge and take responsibility for accomplishing them. If he failed, he could use that failure to determine how to better learn the subject, or improve his study skills. As for his reference to teachers as being "dumb" he was then able to say to himself, "That's the teacher's problem with her own insecurity or personality problem and not a personal reference to my ability."

2. The second story came as a reflective moment during one of my final sessions with a boy who had been seeing me for academic assistance during his last two years of high school. As he reflected on how much he had changed since his first visit with me, he noted that he got thinner, stronger, and even more intelligent. Since thinner and stronger were quite evident and he attributed those changes to maturity, he still could not figure out why his intelligence had significantly changed over the past few years. I asked him to reflect on any situation that may have happened when he was younger that made him feel inadequate. He quickly remembered the time when his teacher held up two papers to show the students what kind of a paper she wanted and what kind of a paper she would consider unacceptable. His paper was used as the example for what NOT to do. From that time on, he felt inadequate as a learner and even as a person. His whole body language displayed one of defeat; he walked with his head down, his body bent over and his verbal comments about himself were always demeaning. Over time, his academic success showed him that he was intellectually adequate and his ability to discuss how much he knew and how proud he was of his accomplishments diminished his poor image and

helped him to subconsciously overcome his feelings of inadequacy. His opportunity to finally face what caused his feelings of intellectual inadequacy helped him overcome his demon and move on with his hard earned success.

As you can see, trigger words are not easily defined. Even the people who hear them do not always know they are going to trigger a response to what you said. Therefore, when we attend to someone in our business, classroom, home, or other environment, we need to try to take a step back from the situation to determine what was actually said and how those words were interpreted in the mind of the listener. Calm exploration as seen in the previous scenarios will help ease the tension and permit the receiver of the words to be able to reflect on the impact specific words have on their past experiences.

Situational Words

A friend wrote to me the other day and told me that her friend's 30-year-old brother had died. She wanted to help her but was unsure how to use her words so as not to open a door which may be a very private place for the grieving person.

My advice was to start with honesty by noting that she had never been involved in the death of a young family member so she was a little unsure of how to console her friend or react to her needs. She should tell her that she wanted to show her concern and love for her by being there to listen to her converse about her brother and to help her heal her wounds of loss. That way, if she said something and her friend started to cry, she could use her empathy for the situation to help her repair anything she felt may have caused her to be uncomfortable.

The following is a situation that happened after Julie's brother died. Mary had been Julie's best friend since they were in high school. She knew Julie's parents very well and wanted to express her sympathy to Julie's parents and offer any assistance they might need. She went over to Julie's parents' house to see if they needed any assistance and found them to be very cold to her. She expressed her feelings to Julie and the conversation transpired as follows:

Mary's Story

Mary: I went over to your parents' house today to offer my help and they were very cold to me. Did I say or do anything wrong?

Julie: Mary, my parents are very upset about the loss of my brother and want to be left alone right now, so please don't go over until you are invited.

Mary: That's fine, please let them know I am here for them and willing to help in any way. Until I hear from them or you,

I will follow your suggestion and wait for either of you to call for assistance. How are you doing with the death of your brother?

Julie: I just can't believe he is dead. I don't know what to say or do right now. I feel numb and don't know how to react.

Mary: Maybe you should just let your body and mind dictate your next move. Sometimes it is a good idea to just let nature take its time to help you get over the shock and pain of his loss.

Julie: Thanks for understanding.

Bilingual Situations

Bilingual situations can also be tenuous because, when a person has a thick accent and they are trying to speak our language, we can make them feel like we are superior to them because we immediately revert to their language in a conversation.

Juan: Hello – day nice today

Suzie: [Suzie recognizes that Juan has a heavy Spanish accent so she answers him by saying] "Si es un día muy lindo." [She speaks with a heavy American accent and she also speaks loudly as if Juan cannot hear her.]

The other thing that people who speak a different language do, without realizing, is to talk very loudly when a person has an accent. They feel that if they talk louder, they will make themselves heard but the problem is not the volume of the language, it is the understanding of the words that are important.

Juan: You like flowers red?

Suzie: Yes, I want those red ones over there! [She raises her voice as she speaks and points to the flowers]

Poor Juan feels uncomfortable because Suzie has called attention to their conversation in two ways; she is raising her voice and correcting his English in front of other people. Suzie probably does not even realize what she has done.

These language nuances tend to either aid or break down relationships as noted by the many scenarios presented throughout the book. Let's look at how Juan and Suzie can repair their differences in the following example:

Juan: Hello – nice day today

Suzie: [Suzie recognizes that Juan has a strong Spanish accent when he talks to her yet, she respects the fact that Juan is trying to communicate in her native language so she continues talking to him in English] Yes, it is a nice day.

Juan: You like flowers red?

Suzie: [She realizes that he made a mistake in English but, rather than correct his English or speak loudly at him, she uses the correct form of sentence structure by saying] Yes, I like red flowers. Do you have three pots of those red flowers?

Juan: [Learns the correct structure from Suzie's language modeling] Yes, I have three pots of red flowers. You want?

Suzie: Yes, I want them. Could you put the red flowers in my car? Thanks!

Juan: No, thank you for buying flowers and for the English lesson! [Both have a good laugh]

We can gain more respect from people of different cultures when we respect the fact that they are trying to learn our language. They are not deaf, nor are they stupid. Put yourself in the place of an English-as-a-Second-Language (ESL) learner. Think how you might sound to someone who is proficient in a language different to yours. After putting yourself in that person's position, you will probably have more empathy and respect for their efforts. Suzie accomplished her goal of correcting Juan's English without having to speak loudly or overtly correcting his language. She just took the words he spoke and answered his question using the correct adjective (red) noun (flowers) format. Juan picked up on Suzie's modeling and was able to learn from her clever assistance.

Situational words are often difficult because we need to delve into the private world of the receiver of our words when we speak them. Sometimes our words can be comforting; other times they may be interpreted differently than we originally intended. Just being sensitive to the situation will help you repair or ignore the reaction.

Eye Secrets

Over the years, I have noted how we use our eyes to convey our messages. The next scenario is an example of how two people felt a lack of discourse because they did not use their eyes to attain and sustain the conversational focus.

One day, a couple came into the office, each complaining that the other person never listened. As I watched them discuss their problem, I noticed that each one looked directly at me and not at each other when they talked. After watching their conversation for a while, I asked, "Why do you think your communication breaks down?" and they could not answer me. Then, I pointed out that I noticed they did not look at each other when they talked with each other. That trivial-seeming point was then used as a talking point from which I helped them understand the importance of using eye contact during interpersonal conversations based on how the brain functions. Dr. Daniel Siegel (1999) wrote the book, *The developing mind; Toward a neurobiology of interpersonal experience* and explains how we connect our minds:

> The obitofrontal cortex – the part of the brain just behind the eyes and located at a strategic spot at the top of the emotional limbic system, next to the "higher" associational cortex responsible for various forms of thought and consciousness—plays an important role in affect regulation. This area of the brain is especially sensitive to face-to-face communication and eye contact. Because it serves as an important center of appraisal, it has a direct influence on the elaboration of states of arousal into various types of emotional experience (p. 280).

In other words, the appraisal of one's discussion and the acceptance by the second party become paramount in facilitating the verbal and nonverbal interactions of both parties. Once the couple understood the important function of using our eyes to facilitate and enhance our interpersonal communication, they agreed to go home and try looking at each other when they spoke.

A week later, the couple returned to the office and noted that their interpersonal communication had improved. With a slight chuckle, we all were able to see how something that seemed as trivial as connecting brains through eye contact enhanced and improved their interpersonal communication! If you don't believe me, think of this. Have you ever stopped at a red light and felt someone staring at you? When you looked over, the person in the car next to you was looking at you! Hopefully, he was tall, dark and handsome or the most gorgeous woman you have ever seen in your life! Whatever the case, you can now understand the power we have in just the mere use of our eyes.

If you reflect on the personal interactions you have had with people today, think about how their eye contact was used and how you felt in response to that contact. Let's think how people use their eyes.

You look directly at the person or play with your glances when you want to:

   ✓ Make a point known

   ✓ Engage in flirting

   ✓ Show your anger or aggression

   ✓ Ask a question

   ✓ Show interest

   ✓ Gather important information

You look down or away when you:

   ✓ Are afraid or ashamed

   ✓ Fear the other person will see what you are thinking

   ✓ Feel vulnerable

✓ Don't want the other person to know what you are doing or thinking

Lack of eye contact can be misinterpreted. The receiver may sense your lack of eye contact and feel you are not interested in what he/she has to say. This prior scenario is a good example of how eye contact detracted from the relationship. When I make this point with people they think this is so obvious, yet, it is one of the last things they check when they complain of communication breakdown. For example, how often are you telling your spouse something and he/she walks out of the room? How do you feel when that happens? Especially when they come back later and tell you that you never told them that!!! Hummm! It was not the words used in that scenario that broke down the relationship but the lack of eye contact that caused the speaker to feel that the listener was not interested in what was being said. The speaker got the impression that his/her words were not as important as whatever the person was thinking because the person put his/her destination (by leaving the room when the other person was talking) as a more important task than the importance of listening to the person speaking. When I mention this type of situation to others, I often get the comment, "How rude!" Yes, it is rude but how often do we all do this to others and never realize we are giving the impression of being rude!

Walking Away and Downshifting

As seen in the prior example, the person did not intentionally walk out of the room but the act of leaving made the speaker feel frustrated. This form of walking away is intentional because your goal is to use the act of walking away as a means of getting the listener to become more responsible or to think about what you have just said.

Why does walking away help the brain to process information? According to Eric Jensen (1998, ASCD *Teaching with the Brain in Mind,* pp. 45-46): "Generally the brain does poorly at continuous, high-level attention."

Jensen explains the process of permitting the brain to have time to consolidate information:

> First, much of what we learn cannot be processed consciously; it happens too fast. We need time to process it. Second, in order to create new meaning, we need internal time. Meaning is always generated from within, not externally. Third, after each new learning experience, we need time for the learning to 'imprint.' (p.46)

If we stick around and continue our banter, the real impact of the process and the product will never be absorbed nor instilled into the person's own system. This may be one reason why people who are constantly "talked to" don't seem to learn from this process, no matter how many times you say it. The information never had time to be distilled within that person's system and the constant "external" input never permitted that person's system enough time to make meaning of the information they gathered so they could individually "imprint" it into their own system.

One day a woman came into my office complaining of the difficulty she had getting her son to clean up his room. She said she got tired of telling him over and over to clean up his room. In desperation, she was going to throw out everything he had and leave only the bare essentials in his room! Before she took such drastic action, I asked her to try the following:

1. Define between both of you what "clean up your room" means to each of you. By doing this, you get an understanding of how each of you interpret that goal. In this particular case, the son thought "cleaning his room" just meant getting the clothes off the floor and into his hamper. Once his mother heard his interpretation, she realized that what she wanted was not what he interpreted. So, getting a mutual interpretation between them was winning half of the battle.

2. Either discuss or demonstrate what a "clean room" is supposed to look like so that all involved are able to feel comfortable when the "clean room" appears.

3. After you set up the initial interpretation of a "clean room" don't stay in the doorway giving the child a lecture each time you want his room cleaned.

4. Rather than tell the son that he needs to clean his room each time you walk past it, just ask a question such as – "What do you think needs to happen with your room?" or "What's wrong with this picture?"

5. Wait for the person to respond. They may say, "I don't know" and you can indicate "do you believe this room is appropriately clean based on our discussion?"

6. Wait for a response such as, "Yeah, I know what to do-you don't have to get on my back."

7. Once you hear the words that explain the task at hand walk away so that person has the opportunity to put those words into action.

8. What if you go by the room and he/she is playing with a toy or talking on the phone for an extended period of time?

    a. Remind them by saying, "what should you be doing right now?"

    b. Or, "I gave you a chance to attend to your room without getting on your back, you CHOSE to ignore that opportunity – so I now shall make a choice for you...I will take away ----privilege today.

9. Expect the room to be cleaned and continue with the reprimand of taking away a privilege. Consistency in reprimands is very important so the child understands that you will stand by your words. If this

situation should occur in the future, your son or daughter will already know what will transpire if they do not follow through with their actions.

It is very important that you set the child up for success rather than failure. That is why the first step is to make sure that both of you are clear on what a clean room is supposed to look like before you start requiring him or her to attain and sustain that goal. Most kids, and especially teenagers, like this type of discussion because they soon learn that they are actually the only person in control of their own life. If they want to be treated with respect and not constantly talked to about their lack of responsibility, just set them up for success and harmony will follow.

One mother who has used this process successfully met me in the supermarket the other day. She noted that this was the BEST summer she had ever had with her kids! No fights and no problems. She said that she does not even have to complete the question because she just starts saying, "Hey, what needs . . . " and her sons will stop her sentence midstream and say, "I know Mom," and the day goes on without struggles or frustrations.

The downshifting glance and walking away can effectively be used in business, education, relationships, and any place you want to make an impact without causing discord. Business people like using questions rather than telling their employees what to do because they soon see the employee taking control of situations without having to be told what to do. This alleviates the need for the employer to constantly be monitoring their work.

To place further impact on the InterActive process, the glance is a nice way of making an impact on a conversation without creating verbal tension.

The Glance

I consider "the glance" as one of the least intrusive communicative structure. When you have something to convey to another person, but are not too sure how that information may be accepted, start your comment with your eyes at a downward or outward gaze while you are beginning your comment. Once you get the basic information off your chest and are ready to make an impact, turn your gaze to focus on the person with whom you are speaking.

The Move Story

One day, a mother came to my office to ask advice on removing her son from a public school and placing him in a private school. She noted that he went to this private school over the summer and she felt it was a lot of fun and very progressive. She felt that moving to this school would be a good choice because he would be more motivated to go to school; therefore, homework and schoolwork would be less of a hassle because he would be very motivated to learn. Before we had a chance to really look at all the options, she made the decision to place him in the progressive private school. After a couple of months, the child was bored and the mother lamented her choice. She noted that she had made a mistake and felt terrible about telling her son who by now, was getting pretty accustomed to going to school and viewed it as an easy play period. Thus, she asked me how she could convey the message to her child that she was going to take him out of this school and return him to his prior educational environment. We role-played the scenario to help her get a feel for how her son would take the news.

Me playing Mom: [Looking at the child] John, come sit by me a second.

Mom playing child: [Looking at her for clarification] Yeah Mom – what's up?

Me playing Mom: [Looking down and not directly into the child's eyes] Remember when you left your old school to go to the new one and we discussed how much fun the new school would be?

Mom playing child: [Looking at mother] Yeah! This school is really fun – we get to play all day! I like it at this school.

Me playing Mom: [Raising my eyes and starting to look at the child to make a point] Well, I'm glad you've had a chance to play at this school but, let's take a quick look at the work you're doing at school. [I show a collection of work we got from the school and note how there is no writing and the math is the same math done last year.] Do you think this work is harder or easier than the work you did at your last school?

Mom playing child: [Looking at the work displayed] Yeah, it looks pretty easy.

Me playing Mom: [Looking at the work for a second then, making eye contact] I agree with you. Do you think this work is challenging or is it kind of easy?

Mom playing child: [Looking at the work] Yeah, it's pretty easy.

Me playing Mom: [Looking directly at child] what do you think about going back to your old school? We both agree that this work is very easy and, although you're having a nice time playing, do you really think you'll be prepared to go into fourth grade next year if we continue at this school?

Mom playing child: [Looking away from Mom] But Mom! Now I'll have to work hard and it will be even harder to catch up than before I left!

Me playing Mom: [Looking at child] I've got an idea! What if we take the next two months, that is November and December, and get you caught up with the work before you start back to school in January? That way, you can continue to go to your new school, but we can get work from your old school and get you caught up with the class at home. If you feel you need more time to work on your schoolwork, I will get permission to home-school you in the afternoon at home.

Mom playing child: [Looking at the floor sadly]

Me playing Mom: [Taking child's chin and turning her head toward the mom] I know you feel that this will be a lot of work, but we can do this together and that way you will be comfortable when you go back to school. We gave this new school a try and it just was not the fit we needed.

Mom playing child: [Looking at Mom] Yes, I guess it will all be better once I get back to my old school and, Mom, I kinda miss my old friends, and maybe this won't be such a bad thing after all.

After role-playing this situation, the mother went home prepared to work through this situation with her child. When she looked at him and started to discuss the pros and cons of staying at the new school, the child told her that he was glad his mom had made the decision because the school was becoming too boring. Although Mom did not have to use the whole practice scenario, just looking at her son and letting him see the truth she was feeling in her eyes seemed to help her son connect with her thoughts.

How to Work Through a Difficult Situation

Let's use the aforementioned scenario to help you understand the process of using your eyes to communicate. This approach has two parts: (1) when you start your comment without looking at the other person, you are giving that person time to think about what you have to say; (2) the next part permits you to raise your glance as a means of slowly moving your thoughts from your mind to connect with the other person's mind. When you actually make contact with the other person's eyes, they are getting the full impact of your statement.

The rationale for this type of eye contact is to slowly approach a tender or sensitive topic without engaging in full eye contact from the onset. This approach gives you time to understand your listener's mood and gives you time to determine how it will be accepted. By the time your eyes meet the listener's eyes, you will have given yourself and the unknown impact to the delicate situation sufficient time to ferret out where you stand, and by not using initial eye connection, you are now able to complete your thoughts.

There are times, however, when you want an immediate and more profound visual impact. Let's explore these situations.

The Full Impact Look

When you have something to say and you want to make sure that the other person does not misinterpret your intentions, keep a full-impact connection throughout the conversation or comment. This type of communication format helps you view the impact of your words while observing the reaction your words are having on the receiver. You can use the feedback you are gaining from that person's body language and words as a means of determining the strength of the words you will use next. If the other person looks like they are receptive to your words, then you can continue using the same power and conviction as when you started. If, however, the receiver of your words seems either upset or confused, you can then use that information to help you determine how to proceed.

The Textbooks Story

A mother finds her son's college textbooks and notebook in the back of the car. She notices that his notebook lacks the previous week's classroom notes. She knows that if her son is not going to class he may be trying to hide something from her. She fears that he may try to lie to her and she does not want to go that route because he has done so in the past and she feels that she needs to nip a possible difficult situation in the bud. Therefore, she will use the electrical system of her eyes to make contact with her son before he realizes that she has suspected his actions.

Mom: Son, I found your books in the car and [looks him in the eyes] I wanted to know why you don't have any notes in your binder from last week.

Son: I missed lab one day because I wasn't able to get a ride to school and the teacher told me she was going to drop me from the class.

Mom: [continues to look at her son but, in a concerned way] Have you missed previous labs?

Son: No. That's just the teacher's rule and I guess I have to abide by it.

Mom: Have you tried talking to the teacher to see if she'll reinstate you in the class.

Son: No, I feel like I'm a loser and I just can't go to class anymore!

Mom: [Looks at son with concern and worry] So, do you want me to intervene?

Son: No Mom, I'm just confused and need time to decide what I want to do about my own education, but thanks for being there for me.

Mom: I hope you know that you can come to me or your dad *before* you think about dropping out of that class. Do you want either of us to go to bat for you?

Son: I'm just glad that you showed me you understand and aren't angry at me for being confused about my future. Thanks for giving me the chance to tell you how I'm feeling right now and, I know you'll be there if I need your help. Growing up isn't as easy as I thought!

Mom: [Gives her son and hug and a comforting look.]

This young man talked to his teacher and they decided to have him drop the class because he was falling too far behind to actually catch up and get a passing grade. He saw this opportunity to drop the class as a means of being given a chance to explore his future educational requirements to change his bad study habits. Just knowing that his parents supported his decision and his personal needs spurred him on to take that class again the following trimester. Although he did not ace the class, he passed it with a decent grade. The best part of this difficult situation was that he started to realize that his parents were human and that they were willing to help him through a difficult time. This situation actually helped the family learn to communicate with each other in ways that were less intimidating and more interactive.

As we revisit the "full impact" scenario, I'm sure most readers thought that a full-on look is only used when you are completely angry and want to show the other person the extent of your anger. However, as seen in the previous scenario, these intense looks can be a deeper way of connecting with the soul of that person. Note, however, that your eyes are judging each possible opportunity to read the situation. When the situation changes, or if the body language of the other changes, so too will your look. The words and body language you use will usually change in accordance with what outcome you want to produce. Let's replay the previous situation with a different outlook.

Mom: [Looks at her son with anger and frustration in her eyes] I saw your books in the back of the car and you are missing last week's notes. Are you off doing drugs or something? Why are you disrespecting your father and me by not going to school?

Son: Ah, no Mom, I just forgot to write any notes. Anyway, why are you so mad at me?

Mom: [Continues with anger in her eyes] Mad! Ha! I'm furious at your lack of maturity and I'm angry that you can't even take a few courses and complete them correctly. Maybe you shouldn't even be going to college! You are so immature; you don't deserve to go to college right now. You wait until tonight and we'll talk with your father on this one!

Son: [His head is down and depressed] I won't be home tonight. Don't worry about me. You only want me to be a good student so you can brag to your friends. Well, sorry I let you down!

As one can see, nothing was resolved in the conversation because the mother's look started the downward spiral of conviction which was then confirmed by her demeaning and accusing words. In order to save face, the son felt he had no other recourse but to stop the conversation and leave home because he felt he was not appreciated, nor was he ever going to have a chance to have his mother believe in him or help him through this difficult time of his life.

As we have seen in the last example, now that you have a general idea of how to use your eyes in a conversation, the next step is to determine how to use your words. The main point here is to think truthfully about the real intention you have in mind when you want your words to make an emotional impact on the person receiving your words.

Truth, Intention, and Emotion

The words truth, intention, and emotion are often intertwined when we get into power struggles with others. We have found that when people are constantly being talked to and told what to do and how to do it, they often "bend the truth" to get away from having to be the recipient of a long discussion about their inappropriate actions or behavior. In order to get away from such behaviors, you might want to think about what your intentions are when you want someone to either change their behavior, or to act in a different way. We often feel that everyone knows what we want and that everyone understands our reactions. However, there is only one person in your body and that is you. So, in order to help the rest of the people with whom you interact to have a better understanding of how you are feeling or what you expect from them, you need to be truthful with yourself by defining your intention(s) and the rationale for using words that usually elicit emotional reaction(s).

The other day the owner of a business came in and was very upset with how an employee continually reacted to her requests for assistance. When I asked her to define what specifically she wanted her employee to do each day, she had great difficulty defining her required tasks. So I asked if she had a job description for her employee so that person would know what was required of her job position. The business owner said that she thought it was quite apparent that the employee should take up the slack when needed. So I asked the owner to define "slack" and she gave me an odd look. Her silence gave me the chance to help her understand that, if the employer could not define "slack", how would the employee be able to go through a day knowing what was expected of her? This comment helped the owner realize that the emotional reaction she was having with her employee stemmed from her lack of defining her intentions and this lack of definition resulted in an emotional turmoil between both employer and employee. Given this and many similar scenarios, we might want to think before we get frustrated with any given situation. Try using these steps:

1. What are my expectations for this employee, family member, peer, or other? Be truthful with yourself and be able to define why you want a certain response to your expectations.

2. Have I made my expectations clear enough so that all involved understand those goals and needs? How much am I keeping in my head by thinking everyone should know what I am thinking and how much am I being open and truthful about my needs and/or concerns?

3. Once these expectations are defined and personally rationalized, discuss how they should be made clear for anyone involved.

For example, should you make up a job description so that all employees know their positions and the boundaries? If so, write them down and give a copy to the employee. If this is a personal issue, be truthful with yourself and define the rationale for your anger, frustration, etc. by telling those involved how you feel and why you are reacting in such a way. For example, I tended to get very nervous, sensitive and easily upset when I was in my premenstrual cycle. During that time of the month, I often blamed others for my own bad mood and aggression. However, after I started being more truthful with myself, I would often tell those around me that this was not the time of the month to be kidding or playing with me because I would probably overreact to anything that was said. Although that was not enough of an excuse to permit myself to be mean to others, just identifying why I was overreacting and being truthful with both myself and others seemed to help me defuse my own anger and aggression. If I did get mad, at least others knew not to take my mood personally. Overall, the bottom line is to respect the fact that other people have feelings and we need to keep that in mind when interacting with others.

Respect

One of the first things that kids say about their parents is, "I don't feel respected." They feel their parents make all their decisions and are constantly on their backs about everything they do. They feel they cannot establish their own personality because their parents keep robbing them of the opportunity to think for themselves. This disrespected feeling can become a source of frustration for the child or teenager.

Parents, on the other hand, feel that permitting a child or teenager to take part in the decision process provides a sign to the child that they will have free reign to start making and breaking rules at will. Parents often feel vulnerable and fear they will lose control of their child or children by permitting them to have a voice in the decision-making process. This actually has not been the case with any of the families we worked with because once a child is respected for his/her ability to make good choices; they want to continue making those decisions. The way they get and continue maintaining that mutual respect is by complying with the mutually acquired goals. Imagine if your boss kept telling you what to do. Each day, you would feel less and less needed and appreciated because you could not make your own decisions. Over time, you would begin to feel like a slave and not an active member of the company.

Imagine another scenario. You start a new job and you and your boss discuss your job requirements. Rather than constantly telling you what to do, the boss praises you for your efforts. However, when you do not know how to do something, he/she respectfully discusses the piece you need to learn. You would feel appreciated and needed because you were accepted as a person with the ability to think and to carry out your job appropriately. This interaction actually makes, not only your job easier, but also easier for the boss. The same holds true for families.

Look at families who seem to have a good working relationship and see how they interact with each other. Do you hear disparaging words such as "stupid" or "You're so dumb?" You probably will not hear much of any aggression or nagging on the members because they are accepted for their intelligence and ability to make appropriate choices.

The homework scenario previously discussed is a good example of how a child can feel disrespected or empowered by the way we use our words and actions. Let's revisit this scenario with a new perspective this time. Let's say the child was supposed to turn off the TV after taking a 30-minute break from studies and he/she continues to watch the television. The mother or father could go in, turn off the TV and yell at the child or the parent could try the following scenario.

Parent: What time is it?

Child answers: 4:30

Parent: So, what are you supposed to be doing at 4:30?

Child reflects: Oops! Homework! You don't need to get on my case. I know what I have to do.

And that is it – end of conversation and problems. If the parent continues to nag the child, nothing will be accomplished. Ask, avoid telling, and see what happens. Many people ask me how to begin this whole process and I tell them to "begin with the end." That means, think about what you want to accomplish with your conversation and plan your conversation with the end result in mind.

Begin with the End

InterActive speech is simplistically defined as the active processing of language between two or more people. Therefore, when we have something to say to another person, define the outcome you want to achieve before you even begin your conversation. By having a defined outcome, you will then be able to be more explicit with your conversational goals. The likelihood of leaving out important information or steps will be lessened because you will then be able to know what you want others to take away from each point in your conversation. A powerful conversation is one that is explicit. This means that there is no room for interpretation of your intentions because the words you use are precise and accurately portray what you want to say. On the other hand, an implicit conversation is one where the words are so general or so open that it leaves the interpretation of those words up to the listener. Implicit conversations are usually filled with questions from the listener asking for clarification of your comments. When I listen to people converse in my office, I tend to formulate a communication plan based on the client's explicit or implicit speech patterns.

Explicit Speech Patterns

People who use explicit speech patterns offer complete thoughts and fill in specific details so that the listener does not have to spend time trying to interpret what was being discussed. To assess your own speech patterns, take a mental note of how many questions the listener has as they hear you talk. If you are talking with someone who does not ask questions, note how effectively your directions were carried out and how precise that person went about the task without requiring redirection or redefinition of your expectations. I tend to equate explicit speech to a good author. The author who writes well will leave no room for interpretation of their work. The intention the author had when writing the work will be the same interpretation the reader will have when the work is read. If that work is well written, anyone who reads it will have the same interpretation of the work that the author had when writing it.

Now, implicit speech patterns leave a lot of room for interpretation. The words expressed are usually global or general terms such as: Do a **good** job. [What does "good" mean to you? Does it mean the same to me?] Or bring **them** to me when you are done. [What does "them" mean? Do you want me to bring all of the envelopes or just the ones going out of the country?]. Implicit speech patterns can obviously be recognized by how many questions people will need to ask you in order to get the task completed correctly. To make this point clear, the following are examples of how explicit and implicit speech patterns can improve or detract from our intended communications.

Explicit and Implicit Conversations

Here is an example of an explicit speech pattern: "The right, front, driver's side, main headlight is out. Could your mechanic replace that bulb? Before it is replaced, however, I need to know how much it will cost to have it replaced and how long it will take for that repair to be done."

Now, using the same scenario, here is an example of an implicit conversation:

Me: I need to get my car fixed

Mechanic: What do you need to have done?

Me: I need to have my light fixed.

Mechanic: Which light?

Me: The one in the front.

Mechanic: What is wrong with it?

Me: It's not working right?

Mechanic: What is it doing? and so on...

Look how long this conversation is taking and I have still not completed telling the mechanic what is wrong with the headlight. We could go on for an hour before we actually get to the problem that needs to be fixed!

How to Carry Out Explicit Speech

Step 1: Determine the specific problem that needs to be addressed.

Step 2: Write down or think of the specific words that will help you describe the location [right, front, driver's side].

Step 3: Determine the specific problem that you want resolved. [The main headlight is out.]

Step 4: Determine who or what is needed to fix it. [The mechanic needs to replace the light.] If you really want to get into more detail you can go to the next step.

Step 5: Ask how much it will cost to have it fixed and how long it will take to have that done.

What if you are uncomfortable with the price? What words will you use to express your concern and have it fixed or will you tell the person that you will look around? All these questions may need to be rehearsed before you even walk into the door of the mechanic's office. By problem-solving in advance, you are now prepared to be the owner of your actions.

How many times have we overpaid for something and kicked ourselves all the way home for letting someone else take over the power of our decision. However, having these problems played out in our mind <u>before</u> the verbal interactions take place will give you the opportunity to determine exactly what you want to do and to carry out your intentions without any pressure from others. Being mentally prepared will help you to either accept or reject the offer based on your predetermined expectations and any possible drawbacks.

All of the above discussions and examples are appropriate for business, relationships, parenting, and social interactions. Business interactions and any structured situation would really benefit from learning how to set the goals expected from employees or groups of individuals. These goals need to be so explicit that anyone who reads or hears the goals will understand what is expected and what outcomes would result from noncompliance. Most business and personal complaints I hear come from the lack of explicit communication. Anyone who interprets the standards for their own inappropriate benefit will possibly cause a rift in the organizational process. Therefore, clarity of thought results in clarity of the spoken word leaving no room for interpretation of the rules.

Explicit Speech – Emotional Planning

The next form of explicit speech pattern involves making your feelings understood to another person. People who have had to make their own decisions and who talk to others throughout their lives are usually pretty comfortable talking about their wants and needs. More often than not, they are more comfortable talking about tangible wants and needs such as fixing their car or getting someone to address an issue at the office. The more difficult piece of explicit speech arises when we need to talk about our own emotional wants and needs such as wanting to be touched or not touched.

Another example relates to wanting someone to just listen to your ranting and not looking for advice because you only want to get an issue off your chest. How are we, who are normally in control of our daily work-related actions going to open our hearts and emotions to permit our most intimate needs to be heard?

Remember the first scenario posed at the beginning of the book? How would you reply to the person who said, "No, you don't love me?" How would you use your eyes and your words to help you work through this scenario? This type of talk is called "implicit speech" because the context is implied and left up to the receiver of those words to interpret the meaning because the words were not specific enough to define all the details of their meaning. Let's play out the scenario:

You: [on the way to the movie with plans for a romantic evening] Hey honey, I love you!

Girlfriend: No, you don't.

You: Because? [As you look her straight in the eyes]

Girlfriend: Because you did not take the dogs to the vet like you told me you would.

You: And lack of doing so tells you that I don't love you?

Girlfriend: Well, it shows you don't care about me.

You: Are the things I do for you considered acts of love?

Girlfriend: Well, yes!

You: So, can I read those words as telling me that you only love me for the things I do for you and not for what you really feel emotionally for me?

Girlfriend: Well, I love you when you help me and when you don't, I feel like I'm unloved.

You: Hmm. To me, love is a deeper feeling of wanting to be with that person no matter what happens. Feeling loved to me means that I am loved for me and not for what I do for you. Do you feel that way?

Girlfriend: Sort of - I guess I could learn to love you like that.

You: Maybe this turned out to be a good conversation after all because now I know where your values lie and I also know that we don't share the same reason for being together.

This couple will have to have more conversations like this to determine where they want to go with their relationship. However, the good news is that they were able to converse. What if you were the type of person who just could not express yourself? You may find that it is the words that you don't use that actually get you into trouble. Therefore, try to be sensitive to how people express themselves, and when you like what you hear, just try to emulate that person's speech patterns. I find speaking to be a similar process to writing; the more you write the better able you are at attaining meaning from the words you write. Again speaking is a similar process. The more you use your words, the better you become at having people understand your intentions by the explicit words you use.

Pulling It All Together

InterActive communication is truly fascinating because we can see from many examples that our lives can be made more peaceful and interactive or aggressive and volatile by simply using the words that come out of our mouths! These six steps, though easy to comprehend, are often more difficult to put into daily practice. The key word here is practice. You will find that success will bring on your own personal success. My own son would hate it when I used it on him because he found that when my husband "told" him to clean his room or do his homework, he could just come back with "I didn't hear you." However, when I asked him a question related to his daily routine such as: "What are you supposed to be doing with your room right now?" He had no choice but to answer my question. For example: when he came home from school, he was supposed to go to the kitchen and complete his homework. If I caught him watching TV instead of doing his homework, the following conversation would transpire:

Me: Should you be watching television right now?

Son: Aggggh! I know, Mom, my homework needs to be done.

Me: Thank you!

Son: [Stomping off to the kitchen.] I hate this dumb way of talking!

Me: Oh, would you rather I treat you like a baby and tell you what to do?

Son: No – I get the message.

You will probably find that using InterActive speech patterns will cause others to get a bit frustrated with you because you are taking the responsibility from your own shoulders and placing it back on the shoulders of others – that is the key and they usually don't like it. Why? Because it is easier to just say they did not hear or that they forgot what you said.

However, when the information you are looking for comes directly from that person's mouth, it goes to their brain and the responsibility is now on that person's shoulders. Over time, you will find that there is less fighting and less repetition of chores or responsibility reminders. The interaction becomes more amicable because there is less anger and frustration between you. Soon, you will find yourself having real conversations with people you might have previously fought with because of inappropriate words or shifting the responsibility onto the other person.

People who have started using this form of communication have not only improved their interpersonal relationships but have also improved interactions with their peers, their workers, their children, and any person with whom they may converse. You can now have a come-back to that rude restaurant server who plops down your food in anger. Or, you can get the person with whom you are speaking to finally open up and tell you what is on his/her mind. Please note that, when you open the door of communication, you also permit the responder to your words to tell you how those words are impacting their thoughts and feelings. This is not a bad omen; however, because – once that door of communication is open, you now know where you stand with the people with whom you are speaking. You now have the opportunity to repair conversations before they cause you to get into a fight or before they result in an uncomfortable situation that you were previously unable to handle.

Overall, everyone who has started using this form of communication has told me that they have such great success, they will never return to their old style of conversing. Teachers and principals who have tried this way of conversing with their students have received comments about being more understanding, more respectful and clearer in their expectations and in their instruction. So, give InterActive speech a try and see for yourself how you can generate positive dynamics in your life solely by using your words! Nothing big to buy, no great program to study – just using this new knowledge is all you need to change your life. Change your language, improve your life!

Bibliography

Jensen, E. (1998). <u>Teaching with the brain in mind.</u> Alexandria, VA: Association for Supervision and Curriculum Development.

Jensen, E. (2005). <u>Teaching with the brain in mind.</u> (2nd ed.) Alexandria, VA: Association for Supervision and Curriculum Development.

Kozulin, A. (1990). <u>Vygotsky's psychology: A biography of ideas.</u> Massachusetts: Harvard University Press.

Siegal, D. (1999). <u>The developing mind; Toward a neurobiology of interpersonal experience).</u>New York: The Guilford Press.

Sylwester, R. (1995). <u>A celebration of neurons: An educator's guide to the human brain.</u> Alexandria, VA: Association for Supervision and Curriculum Development.

Appendix A

Case Studies

Read through the different cases described here and note how those petty instances that play out throughout our days add up to making our daily lives comfortable or pure hell.

The Boss

Mr. Richards is a pretty nice guy. He dresses well, smells good and always has a smile on his face, but why don't his employees like him? Well, I just overheard him talking with Mary, an employee who has been with him for the last 15 years, and the conversation went like this:

Mary: Get me the Gibson file – he says as he rushes in front of her desk.

Mary brings the file and asks: Do you want me to call Mr. Gibson for you?

Mr. Richards: What do you think I am dumb or something? I have fingers and can call him when I'm ready.

Mary: I just wanted to see if you needed some help.

Mr. Richards: If I wanted a mother, I would have my mother working in your place.

Mary feels like she is being put down by Mr. Richards all the time and Mr. Richards feels like Mary is always trying to meddle in his life. Over the years, the words have become a harbor of thoughts without a boat to guide them to shore. The result is two people who have a love/hate relationship. They have learned to live with each other because they need each other, but their days are filled with pain and frustration.

Improving Communication Using InterActive Speech

The Boss

After the incident with "The Boss," Mary asked how that type of situation could be handled using InterActive speech.

Mary: Mr. Richards, does my job description indicate calling clients and addressing the needs of my boss? [Step #1]

Mr. Richards: Yes, why?

Mary: Well, when you asked me to bring the file and I asked if you wanted me to call Mr. Gibson, which should be part of my job description, right? [Clarification of Step #1]

Mr. Richards: True, but this time I want to call him.

Mary: How could you have noted that without making me feel offended? [Step #2]

Mr. Richards: O.K. but, I feel you are always trying to meddle in my life. [Clarification of #2]

Mary: Would you like to discuss either a change in my job description or would you like to let me know which files are personal and which ones are for general business? [Clarification of Step #1 and Step #4]

Mr. Richards: Let's make a drawer in my office for my personal files and leave the business files out in your office. Why didn't we think of these years ago? [Step #1]

Mary: Maybe the next fifteen years will go smoother if we just tell each other what we feel and what we need. That way we won't have to worry about stepping out of line. [Step #1]

Mr. Richards: Great idea!

Mary and Mr. Richards only got through a few steps because their problems are embedded in many years of not using their words to express their wants and needs. This conversation is a good start but they will need to start using the steps daily in order to forge a good working relationship.

The Word-Robbing Family

One day a Teenager entered my office, quickly plopped down and slouched into the corner of the long couch. Although there was plenty of room on the couch, her mother sat on a chair across from her and the father grabbed a chair from behind my desk. Her father started talking about his daughter's problems in school. Each time the daughter tried to tell her side of the story, the father told her to wait until he was finished with his comments. That comment made the young lady pull her coat even closer to her chest and hold her arms tightly around herself. Mom's eyes kept moving from her daughter to her husband trying to determine how to intervene. Finally, the father stopped discussing how he viewed his daughter's problems and his daughter tried to provide her side of the story. About half-way through her interpretation of her academic issues, her mother stepped in to add her comments. As soon as mother took over, the child went back to cuddling her coat and looking down at the floor. No eye contact was made among any of the family members until dad took over the conversation from the mother. The mother gave a cold look at him, which he ignored and continued speaking. This round-robin of lost words continued for about fifteen minutes. By the time I stopped the never-ending rally of unending sentences, all family members were holding their folded arms closely to their chests. From an outsider's perspective, my first act was to break the icy-cold ambience by explaining how each person robbed the words from the other. This action in turn, caused the daughter to feel powerless and completely frustrated.

Once they realized the effect their words had on each other, we were able to examine the various issues that evolved in the short time they were in my office.

It was incredible to see how much each family member wanted to help the other but, in trying to help, each person just made the situation worse and more difficult each time they robbed the words from the other person. I have watched similar situations over the past 35 years and wondered how we could make life easier for everyone by just changing the way we talk to each other. Hence, I set off on my quest to watch people discuss their differences. I started to listen and to ask questions about the words and gestures that were said or interpreted during and after tumultuous discussions. My main goal was to find out why interpersonal interactions prospered or withered.

Improving the Situation Using InterActive Speech

Parent: I'd like to have a family meeting with you so we can help our daughter improve in school. Jane, please help us by telling us what is difficult for you at school so we can get some advice.

Daughter: Well, I'm good at getting my homework done, but I never seem to be able to pass any tests and . . . [dad interrupts his daughter]

Dad: I see her doing her homework . . . [Dr. O stops him from continuing by asking a question]

Dr. O: Excuse me, but your daughter was talking. Do you want to have her explain her problems or are you choosing to talk for your daughter?

Dad: Well, I want you to see what we see at home.

Dr. O: I think I see what is happening at home. Each time your daughter says something you feel is wrong or an inappropriate strategy, you tell her what to do. When she gets to school, she is unable to take tests because she does not have you or Mom beside her to tell her what to do during the test. Let's try this again and let your daughter explain her difficulties and needs.

Dr. O: Let's go to the table and start our work.

Parents: Do you want us to come with you?

Daughter: Yeah, I guess you can see what she's teaching me in case I forget it when I get home.

Dr. O and the daughter use the session to talk about what she knows and what is hard for her to learn. After that, she has the daughter interpret the lesson by showing her how she would use these strategies in her next lesson. Her parents watch the process and permit their daughter to take the leading role in discussing her needs. When the session ended the following discussion transpired:

Dr. O: Well, how do you think your daughter did in being able to define her needs and attend to them?

Mother: I didn't know she was that able to talk about her own stuff. At home she doesn't act that way.

Dr. O: Why do you think that is?

Mother: I guess, after seeing this lesson, that we keep interrupting her and she doesn't get a chance to tell us what she needs.

Father: Well, I noticed that you waited until she came up with an answer and sometimes that was a pretty long wait. My wife and I don't seem to do that.

Dr. O: What have all of you learned from this session?

Mother: I learned to ask more questions. [Step #2]

Father: I noticed that you didn't judge her when she talked. You just listened to her. [Step #4]

Mother: I noticed that, when she couldn't seem to express herself, you used extension words to help her completely define what she wanted and needed. [Step #5].

Daughter: I like it when you used the last thing I said to start your reply to me. That made me feel like you were really listening to me and, if you misunderstood me; I could tell you what I really meant to help you understand what I was trying to tell you. [Step #6]

We did not use all the steps in this situation because it was unnecessary. This family has some habits to break and they will need to form new ones. This session today showed them that they can overcome aggression and frustration when they really listen when each one talks and they can use the steps to help them work through difficult conversations.

The Stepparents

Jean and John were very much in love and both had children from their previous marriages. When they married, they thought it would be great to bring up a "Brady Bunch." However, the two of them each had a different way of bringing up their children and neither knew the extent of the personal history the children had experienced before both of them got together. Therefore, when the parents try to discipline the children, they tend to run to their birth parent for advice and council. The children also felt they were not understood by the parent who was new because the parent used words and comments that made them feel uncomfortable. In essence, there is no common language. How did the Brady Bunch learn how to live together or maybe we should explore how they talked to each other?

Improving the Situation Using InterActive Speech

Before any family interaction takes place, both parents need to:

1. Sit down and determine what problems need to be resolved. They should write them down no matter how trivial they may sound.

2. Use step # 4 to attain a list without fighting or frustration.

3. Come up with a set of rules or boundaries that they feel are important for the family to function [Step #1]

4. Have a family meeting and go back to the first two items to get the children's input without discussing your findings. That way, you will be able to hear their

concerns and possibly come up with new ideas you had not thought of earlier.

5. Compile your list of findings with those of the children – you might want to use a large board or paper so everyone can view each other's comments and concerns.

6. Use the combined list to discuss which items are important to all members of the family and which ones were actually resolved through this family discussion.

7. Write a list of new boundaries [Step #1]

8. Write the remaining steps down and discuss how they can be used in the new family dynamics.

9. Try to actively attend to these steps until they become integrated into the family routine.

10. Have periodic family meetings to discuss how things are going and to make any changes in the boundaries previously established.

The Friends

Mary, Max, Ed, and Jane have been friends from birth. They went to the same schools and continue to keep in touch with each other. As they grow, so do their experiences. However, every once in a while, someone will talk about a confidential situation that proves embarrassing – but you don't know how to talk about it without either getting into a fight or hurting that other person's feelings. What words can you use to put the person in her place and still remain friends without fighting?

Improving the Situation Using InterActive Speech

1. Use empathy to show that person that your intentions are not to get into a fight or cause discord within group members. [Step #3]

2. Ask clarification questions to make sure you had made it clear to that person that you did not want personal information shared with others in the group [Step #2]

3. Once you found out that the person made a mistake and told personal information without your permission, don't point fingers and judge them [Step #4].

4. To get down to more specific information and deeper discussions, use extension words. [Step #5]

5. Set group boundaries so all in the group agree on how personal information should be treated. [Step # 1]

6. Continue using all steps in future discussion so that you can have an open flow of communication without hard feelings. When something comes up again, use the steps to help walk you through better communication and improved interpersonal relations.

The Couple

Jen and Jack have been married for five years. Jen feels that Jack has grown too comfortable with their relationship. He forgets to do nice things for her and expects to come home and have sex whenever he gets in the mood. Jen wants to tell him about her needs but knows that they will end up in a fight with both shutting down. So, rather than fight, both parties just go on being angry at each other. Both are beginning to feel they have lost their love for each other and are contemplating divorce. How can they start to use their words to bring themselves back together and rekindle the fire they once had?

Improving the Situation Using InterActive Speech

1. Set conversational boundaries before you both start to discuss what is wrong with your relationship [Step

#1]. For example, before we begin, let's try to talk about what really bugs each of us when we try to discuss, like raising voices, walking away etc.

2. When you feel that the other person is wrong or changing the subject, ask, don't tell them what you want them to do [Step 2]. For example, the other person starts to raise his/her voice. Ask, "Do you have to raise your voice to me?" "Let's just try to talk this out so each person has a chance to be heard. [Step #3]

3. Listen without judging because you don't know everything about the other person's past nor are you in his/her body and you don't know how your actions and reactions are really impacting that person. [Step #4]

4. When the other person gives a nebulous or unclear answer, use extension words to help clarify that person's intensions. For example, "You get mad because. . . "Then wait for answer. If you get a fragmented or partial answer continue with extension words such as, because . . . so . . . therefore. . . to help that person get down to clarifying the issue or problem.

5. To help the other person know you are really listening, use the last word or concept they say. For example: "When I go to bed and turn over without saying good night, I do that because you never show me any affection when I am sitting on the couch or when I come home from work." [Step #6]

This couple could use all steps in a sequential order to attend to their problems because their problems seem to flow from one issue to the other and all steps are needed to help the relationship improve.

The Boy Scouts

The big overnight weekend had arrived and all the boys took turns working toward their badges. The scout leader noticed tension with one of the boys (John). Before he could go up to ask what was wrong, he caught John punching Jim in the face. Upon further examination he found out that the other scouts were picking on John. Finally, John could not take it any longer and just exploded. The scout leader took the two boys aside and told them how to behave at camp. He explained how their actions were inappropriate and told them they needed to learn how to interact without hitting or punching. He talked with the rest of the boys in the group and told them not to bully others and to respect each other. After the discussion, the boys went on their way leaving John by himself for fear of either getting into trouble or getting hit by him.

How would you have handled this situation? Do you think the boys understood the problem and were they able to improve their behaviors?

Improving the Situation Using InterActive Speech

1. The Boy Scout leader did all of the talking for the boys. Before they started their trip they should have talked about situations that have happened in past years and had the boys help the Scout leader devise boundaries or rules to be used on the current trip. [Step #1]

2. When the boy lost control and punched the other boy in the mouth, the leader should have asked the boys to join the circle to discuss the issue. Before they began the discussion, he should have discussed the steps to help set the ground rules for the discussion. [Steps 1-6 in brief overview]

3. As each boy talked, he should have asked questions to help the boy define the problem. If he got stuck, he should have used extension words to help the boy continue the conversion on in a logical and sequential way. [Steps 2, 5 and 6]

4. When a boy started to accuse and become aggressive, he could have asked the boy how he could rephrase that so the other person learned from the situation without feeling offended. [Steps 3 & 4]

5. After both boys had a chance to discuss their issues, he could have gone back to the Boy Scout manual and discussed how their behavior and newfound ways of talking facilitated the points discussed in their manual. That way, all boys at camp that day could have learned a lesson on friendship, loyalty, and communication.